# Contents

# INTRODUCTION

Why write a short story that is 100% centered around politics? Isn't that the one subject, well, that and religion, that you weren't supposed to discuss in a polite society? But it seems that's certainly been thrown out the window, along with the phrase "polite society".

But wait, I WANT to be polite. My parents taught that to me. So did Mr. Rogers and Dale Carnegie. Despite my (and yours) lapses into hysteria over something new the government is either doing or failing to do, you still want to be nice. No, I do not want to see homeless and hungry people on the street. Sweep them into another city so I can't see them. Okay, that's a joke, but we must joke. It's what's in your heart that counts, and I don't want to see homelessness and hunger, or to know it exists, or sick people, especially when they don't have the means to get well. But I also remember the story about the squirrels, one who worked all fall, from morning to night, gathering acorns for the summer, while the lazy squirrel played all day. The industrious squirrel warned him several times, and yet, when the snowstorms came in the winter, the lazy squirrel had to beg for help from the well-fed squirrel. He could help, but only a little, because he had a family, and had to put their interests and well-being first. The moral? Well, of course, it's "be prepared", "be responsible". Is the moral, "you must help others?" No, that's not the moral. Not here. It assumes the squirrel that prepared is decent, but how far does decency extend? Does his own family suffer? And how much should the squirrel give to the hungry squirrel? That's up to him, isn't it? The prepared squirrel, has that right, doesn't he? And could we blame the "prepared squirrel" for feeling a little bitter if he was forced to give to the hungry squirrel? He remembered all the wild squirrel parties he had to miss so that he could take care of his family. And if some "Squirrel Parliament" decided that he had to give most of his acorns to the government, well then, why put in as much effort? Or any at all? Especially if the hungry squirrel would get the same amount of acorns, for doing nothing. The result? Not enough squirrels gathered acorns and the entire squirrel kingdom died from starvation the next winter.

The REAL moral? Well, there's more than one, I suppose:

> ➢ Be prepared.
> ➢ Put in the work, do your best.
> ➢ Take some help if you need to, but as soon as you're able to, do your part. Give back.
> ➢ If you decide not to work because you'd rather play, somebody else will take care of you, through a government mandate.
> ➢ Due to human nature, sooner or later, when everybody decided they didn't want to work, everybody would die.

You know, I didn't plan to take that to any specific area, you know, look too liberal or too conservative. I simply wrote about it, and it suddenly took care of itself.

That's the story of Milt Greenbaum, the central character to my story, "The Phantom Candidate". A good man by all accounts. Loving son, hard worker, smart and industrious. He believes that the best way to govern is by getting people together instead of hating the opposition and hoping you win by one vote. No, Milt thought like the industrious squirrel. Work hard, take responsibility, and help others all that you can while still living a good life with your family. Milt has been extremely active in the community, raising funds with the Kiwanis Club and other organizations. But he also believes that the country needs bulldogs, men/women of industry, thinkers, inventors, and people chasing riches. These people move the nation forward. Workers are great and needed, but we move ahead thanks to dreamers that turn those dreams into action, of moving forward for the betterment of all. And make them pay taxes but reward their status through a lower rate. That sounds radical, but we always have a handful of radical views.

I don't know why people with different opinions both can't be good people, simply with another opinion on how to do things in this world. And yes, sometimes we scratch our heads, wondering how they, or anyone (any "smart person", naturally), could believe as they do, instead of the way that YOU do (the correct way, the truth). You can be a little frustrated with them. That's okay, but you know they're typically smart, so you simply must acknowledge their viewpoint, without understanding or agreeing with it. But it's hard, especially with the advent of social media. Our candidate, Milt, will face continuous criticism, nasty comments, many times because we were looking for mutual agreement, or compromise. We explain why Americans don't want compromise, so why would anyone ever vote for a candidate who wanted both sides to come out with something.

So, in writing this, I open myself up to almost *everybody* hating me for what I wrote, because of the personality I gave to Governor Milt Greenbaum. Well, it's a story. Nobody likes boring any more than taxes.

I wish the world was more like Andy Griffith on his 60's show. He wanted to be friendly, to smile, to help, but sometimes, he couldn't. It calls for seriousness. He probably wouldn't comment if somebody else's child was up to something, but when it came to his own son, Opie, he would parent, and Opie would be taught a lesson. When Opie loses his foot race, Andy didn't go out and buy him a medal. No, Opie had to learn about losing, sometimes, in life.

Good or bad, I don't get a lot of readers for my books and stories. I wish that would change, but at least it keeps the criticism down. Hope you enjoy this "medium length story". You're likely to agree with some things and disagree with others. You'll have to decide if that's right or not.

# The Family Story

Milt Greenbaum isn't sure exactly, the details of his family's immigration to the U.S. It's sketchy, and he has always been curious. But through his questions, there are some things he has been able to string together.

His Great Grandparents immigrated through Charleston as very young children, from Lithuania. His father's side had the name "Chernyakhovsky", but somehow, the officer that day in Charleston never got it right, and he gave them a name he had heard earlier in the day, Greenbaum. And that was that. Who was to argue? They were in America.

Though the families always stressed the value of learning, of studying the Torah, they had to make a living, mostly, as farmers in the old country. However, Milt's Great Grandfather, Isidore, came to realize that being a produce merchant had great benefits. Instead of traveling long distances to markets like Memphis, Isidore Greenbaum started his own market, naturally, "Greenbaum's" in Clarksdale, MS. Why Clarksdale? Well, word of mouth, mostly. A few Jews, mostly merchants, got word back that it's not a bad place to live, no pogroms, no violence yet against Jews, just the usual comments here and there that you must expect being different. You work hard, you treat people fairly, and you persevere. After all, people must eat, literally, so why not make a life in the grocery industry?

Greenbaum had customers from the entire area, as far north as Tunica and as south as Cleveland. But the real money was in Memphis, and eventually, Greenbaum's son, Benjamin "Benny" Greenbaum started hitting the southern areas of Memphis. By 1936, when Benny was just twenty-three, Greenbaum's had 16 stores in Memphis and was known as Memphis's Grocery store.

Benny continued a long-standing tradition of offering free boiled peanuts in the front, and a cup of RC Cola.

For many years, due mostly because of the family's love of the town, offices for Greenbaum's remained in Clarksdale.  Milt's Dad, Robert, or "Robbie" Greenbaum, used to tell Milt stories of growing up in Clarksdale. Days hanging out at the Woolworth's on Yazoo Avenue, going to see movies at the Paramount Theater, and of course, working at the original Greenbaum's, near the corner of Desoto and North State Street. Clarksdale was famous for being the "birthplace of the blues", and musicians like Muddy Waters, John Lee Hooker, and Robert Johnson all spent time there. Many of the merchants in the early part of the 20$^{th}$ century were Jewish; owning dry goods stores, and even a restaurant called the "Sanitary Café", that served gefilte fish. Jews lived good lives, with very little antisemitism reported, as long as they accepted the racial attitudes of the time, which most did, probably out of necessity, although it was said that the Black residents showed some favoritism toward the Jewish merchants, preferring to shop in their stores when they could.

Isidore "Izzy" Greenbaum was one of the original founders of Clarksdale's first and last synagogue, Kehilath Jacob, later "Temple Israel", at 69 Delta Street, when he was thirty-four and already well-established as a businessman in the area. By 1929, when the temple moved to a larger location on Catalpa Street, he was President of the Congregation and a key participant in the new building project. He was a good friend of A.H. Freyman, who offered financial support to Jews and non-Jews, and even officiated services.

However, as Greenbaum's continued to grow outside of Clarksdale, Robbie, now given the reigns of the business at the age of just thirty, finally made the difficult decision to move the family eighty miles to the north. When Milt was three, in 1970, the family moved up to the Memphis suburb of Germantown, although he continued to offer financial assistance to Temple Israel, and would often drive down to events, for many years. It simply made sense to have the offices now in Memphis, for the talent pool, as college-educated people preferred the amenities that Memphis could provide, far over Clarksdale. They eventually joined a reform temple in Memphis as well.

Under Robbie's care, Greenbaum's simply exploded. It was time to move into Nashville and Louisville, and by 1986, Greenbaum's had 119 stores and was a regional powerhouse.

Milt worked at the stores as long as he could remember, but it wasn't where he saw himself, and Robbie knew it from their many conversations. Milt had grown to 6'2" and loved to play football, and lift weights. He was personally proud that he had gotten his arm size up to 17 inches, which would grow to 19" by the time he finished playing linebacker for the University of Memphis Tigers, in 1985. He was a starter in his junior year, and 2nd team all-conference, though a life in professional football was not in the cards. It was that same year when Kroger made an offer to Robbie, only fifty-five, but without a son to take over the family business, he was ready for travel and philanthropy. Being a relatively young man, and in good health, it seemed like a dream come true. Milt would get all the financial aid he needed to attend law school, which he did, at Emory, in Atlanta, and of course, with the enormous windfall of the grocery store sale, one day, inherit the family riches.

Sometime during Milt's law school days, he met an Army Officer who was part of the Army's JAG Corps, or "Judge Advocate General's Corps".

After his graduation from Emory, and after passing the Georgia Bar exam, Milt attended the Direct Commission Course (DCC), and the Judge Advocate Officer Basic Course (JAOBC). He became immersed in military law and learned every aspect of the JAG Corps' organization, function, and mission. It was a great fit for Milt. Many of his comrades loved to stay fit and even compete in different sports. Milt kept up his weightlifting and enjoyed hiking the many trails that he traveled to, that different bases took him. He even spent time in Germany.

Milt was a thinker and began to think of his future. He loved the Army, and while he didn't speak about it to anyone, he knew that he would never have to worry about money. He and his dad were very close, and his father believed that a huge stash of money was a "career killer", something that would cause Milt to slack off, questioning hard work and going the extra mile, if he was sitting with a few million dollars in the bank. No, his parents would never allow him to go homeless, go hungry, and not get care, but he needed to live as if his entire life, his livelihood was up to him. In his hands. He asked Milt if he understood that. Many parents in their position believed they were doing their children a favor when the opposite was true. This was why Robbie, Milt's dad, loved the idea of law school combined with the Army. Discipline, a trade. A way to springboard a distinguished Army career into private practice, which is exactly what Milt wanted to do, but there were other things he never told his dad. Milt felt this great country of America, one that had given his family so much opportunity, was slipping. He didn't have specific plans, but he felt that maybe one day, if he continued to work hard, perhaps he could leave a private law practice while still relatively young and run for an office somewhere. Where? What? Maybe Congress? Who knows? He would plant the seed and let it germinate for several years. He was only 27 and just getting started in the Army.

Milt enjoyed a wonderful Army career, and more than once, he was convinced to stay in the JAG Corps, just as he was contemplating moving on. In fact, when he finally got around to it, he was 39, with the rank of Major, and had just completed 12 years in the Army. He had quietly been paying attention to offers in the private sector and had gotten married when he was 36. It didn't take long for he and Debbie's first baby, Bev, to arrive. Two years later would come Adam. Debbie wanted to put down roots, and an attractive offer came to him in Atlanta. He liked the fact that this practice had connections with the political arena in and outside the city. So, in 2006, Milt went to work in the legal offices of Brinkman, Munson, and Kline. Due in part to his skill and his long tenure in the service, practicing law, Milt became a partner four years later, at forty-three.

Milt quietly began to become involved in different civic events. He lived in the Vinings area of Atlanta. It wasn't an incorporated town, but it seemed that every residence and business close enough to the area liked to say that they resided in Vinings. It was upscale, right near the Cumberland offices of the firm, yet with the Chattahoochee River and pretty trails nearby. Milt would find himself on school boards, as a member of the local Kiwanis Club, and heading up other projects and groups. He would be Major Greenbaum whenever it served his purposes, or the group's purpose. At first, and for most of his civic duties, Milt took a very center-of-road approach to his leadership and participation. He tried to help make the local schools safe and effective, and helped raise money for medical facilities through the Kiwanis and other organizations, especially health and nutrition causes through the Kiwanis Club.

Milt was an overachiever and came from a family of overachievers. Running a grocery store was hard work, long hours, let alone running a large chain with over 100 stores. It took a lot of commitment, as did the military, and learning the law. Yet at the same time he believed in doing things for others. Still, he ultimately found himself voting for Republican candidates, because he saw them working on charitable causes as much as anybody else, but their belief was that where your charitable dollars went should be your own decision. He respected the government. After all, he spent all those years in the Army. He realized that the country needed a government, but Capitalism also contributed much. He felt that Capitalism mixed with some social programs was the ideal mix, but it had to be carefully regulated so that the bureaucrats didn't become too powerful.

After six years working at Brinkman, Munson, and Kline, Milt's father passed away from cancer. It happened in Memphis, and it was so fast that it simply shocked everyone that knew Robbie, and everybody in Memphis, Nashville, and Louisville knew Robbie. It was 2010 and Robbie was seventy-five. Four years later, his mom passed away at the age of seventy-seven.

Milt's kids were only seven and nine when Milt turned forty-nine, and with millions of dollars in the bank, much from his parent's inheritance, though Milt had done more than fine over the years, he began to think of a life away from the law, and he didn't really have to ask himself what that might be. It was his tenth anniversary at the firm, and twenty-two years practicing law. He was ready to move on and decided to aim high right from the get-go. He got together with friends at his home, to inquire about a run for the Governorship of Georgia. He had impeccable credentials, aside from being a Jew, of course, but Sam Massell was a Jewish Mayor of Atlanta. Maybe Milt could take it further.

So, in 2016, Milt ran and *won* the Governorship of Georgia. Of course, much is being left out here, such as the constant campaigning, the "Jewish" question in a deep southern state, which turned out to be a non-issue (as least in polite circles), as Milt was a Republican in a red state, at least for the moment. Milt made no effort to hide his service, and why not? His charitable work, love for football and the South. He was still a very big guy and let those meat hook arms get photographed for the front page of the Atlanta Journal Constitution on Sunday, with the caption, Major Milt Greenbaum: Ready to put some muscle back in Georgia Politics (whatever that meant, it sounded good).

Milt ran for two terms, and by 2023, as Milt turned fifty-six, rumors were already flying around about a Presidential bid. Milt did little to dissuade the public, because by now, he wanted it. He felt he was ready, and he let the Republican leadership know that he was on board. Milt was friendly and always watched his words carefully, always good for politics, but things were changing, and Milt didn't like the direction of the country. The USA, once the first line of defense against hated Communism, saw students marching in the streets, demanding Socialism. "These kids", thought Milt, have no idea what Socialism can do to a nation, understanding, still that some social programs were necessary. It was never "all or nothing", but the country was founded on principles of individualism and responsibility that Milt believed was beginning to erode. What happened to "rugged individualism" that settled the wild west? Milt knew all too well the ugly stain of slavery, of civil war, of "Jim Crow" laws and racism, and yet, he was proud of how the country had improved on so many fronts, thanks to brave people who fought back, and some who lost their lives, as is often the case when it came to overcoming bigotry. Milt himself was part of the "Big Brother Program" at Memphis for all four years, taking his "little brother", who was black, to the swimming pool, to sleep in his athletic dorm room, for meals, and always, for at least one additional friend. He was proud of that, and always felt badly that after graduation, he lost touch with Patrick.

Milt felt that most everyone needed a helping hand from time to time, but that we had to strive to make the most of ourselves, to work hard, present yourself well, learn all that you could. If you received help, it should be with the understanding that you "paid if forward". You got back on your feet, and you helped others. But he found people believing ideals that were simply foreign to his thinking, that people should receive a "Basic Universal Income". That meant money for doing nothing. Laying around. He could just hear his father bellowing from downstairs, "Milt, get that lazy butt out of bed and get dressed for work". No work was beneath a man if it was done to the best of their ability. Milt talked to the garbage man as he did another lawyer. With respect. Both worked. Did one have more education, and, let's face it, maybe be more articulate, be able to solve problems better? Yes, of course. People had different levels of problem-solving ability, and I.Q., but if a man or woman did their best to help themselves and society, they deserved respect and a sense of dignity. But the world was changing, and for the worse. Oh yes, gay people could marry, and Milt was open to those kinds of things. A Libertarian stance on most issues. Live and let live, but the reliance on government, and a penchant for revenge, as was the case in some racial issues, were going to simply hurt the nation. Kill it. He was against anything that wasn't merit-based, and against blaming people for the sins of their grandfathers. So, Milt formed an election committee and hired a well-seasoned campaign manager. He made a series of videos, got onto all the social media platforms, and made his announcement to the press.

# The Announcement

*(Atlanta, GA). Two-term Republican Governor Milton Greenbaum of Georgia, a retired Army Major and former attorney, announced his plans to run for the Presidency, a move anticipated by many in and outside of Georgia. Considered a moderate Republican, Greenbaum, a native of Memphis, is also the heir to the Greenbaum Grocery Store chain, once a chain of over 100 stores, before selling out to the Kroger company. Experts and those with ties to Greenbaum say that he is a moderate who feels that the shift left in the Democratic Party may have him viewed as hard right-winger, but that he's frustrated with the direction of the country. All sides of an issue must be discussed freely, and sometimes, compromises made, instead of what he calls "the instant desire to hurl insults, and institute the terrible new practice of 'cancel culture'". A speech in front of the Georgia State Capitol Building is scheduled for tomorrow at 2:00 PM.*

It was overcast, but no rain, when Governor Milton Greenbaum stood up to the podium, with many of the city's well-wishers there to greet him. By now, he had his share of detractors on the other side of the aisle, who would be glad for his inevitable departure from Georgia state government but would be even less happy to see him in the Oval Office.

Milt politely hushed the crowd with his left hand. Eventually, the crowd noise lessened and allowed Milt to speak:

"Well, what a great crowd, but nothing less than I would expect from my many great Georgia friends, and I have them from each part of the state, and believe it or not, each side of the aisle!  I have done my best for Georgia, my adopted state since my Emory days long ago. We've been a Georgia family for a long time, where our kids Bev and Adam call home, and where

Debbie and I both attended college at one point and have loved virtually everything about Georgia. What we didn't love, we've worked hard to change, and I'm prouder of Georgia than ever before!

It's time for us to take our success here in Georgia national. You know, my Republican colleagues have, over the years, accused me of being too close to the center, and perhaps that has been the truth, for a time, but as you know, the differences in the two major parties have widened, and now, without me budging on a single issue. To some, I'm a radical right-winger, prompting some laughs from the partisan crowd.

For me, it's simple. I love this country, and the freedoms associated with it, and I love the United States Constitution. That was always good for a pause and a round of soft applause. I believe in freedom for all. I believe in personal responsibility, of striving to do your best, and I believe in the American people, and their willingness to help others in need. We can be a driven, free, Capitalist nation without being cruel, without being undisciplined, without bigotry or racism, and we can reach out, as individuals or as groups, to help those that need it. My father was my personal hero, and I cannot tell you the number of times he helped feed needy people and gave them jobs. From our little family market in Clarksdale, Mississippi, my dad, grandfather, and great-grandfather helped countless people. For them, a helping hand was more important than a dollar. The dollars would come. And treating people with the same dignity and respect was taught to us every single day. We were in a minority, ourselves.

This country was built on the backs of laborers, and the promise that "all men are created equal". Well, somewhere along the way, or from the very beginning, we failed to adhere to that promise, especially here in the South, but I'm glad to live in a country that can see the error of its ways, and change. We're still a work in progress, but there are black clouds. Clouds of warning tell us that in our zeal to establish a more perfect union, we are taking steps backward. Remember, "You cannot fight injustice with more injustice. Only with justice."

Crimes, and yes, I believe the way we have treated some people in our history was criminal, but it cannot be fixed by advancing the same, or similar treatment to the ancestors of those responsible for the crimes in the first place.  In my Presidency, all will be treated the same. We won't forget the past, we will teach it, but we will live in the present time. We will give, but everybody will be expected to do their best, to work if they are able, to pay a fair share of taxes, and to that extent, I will be looking at alternative tax plans, including the Fair Tax, based on consumption, which has been proven by experts to collect the necessary funds needed to run our government, while eliminating loopholes for the wealthy without punishing them for their success. Nothing is more anti-American, as we are a nation of achievers.

I'll be travelling around our beautiful nation and speaking to countless groups, and I will give honest, unwavering opinions on how I believe our country should be run. My opinions won't change to satisfy the whims of one group, only to change when speaking to a different group. Some of my ideas will seem harsh. I'll be called a spoiled rich kid, a racist, a bigot, and with respect to my religious faith, perhaps even worse things, but I'll won't waver from what I believe to be the truth.

My opponents will come after me, but I will do as I have always done. I'll take the high road. I'll speak my mind and disagree, but I'll look for common ground. The art of compromise seems to have abandoned us here in America. It's "my way or the highway" that seems to be the mantra, and both sides will accuse me of being weak, and not taking a stand, and that's because they will be scared. Scared of my strength and scared that you, the American people, will see through their divisiveness. We are one people but with many ideas, and we must work together. We also must sacrifice at times and be ready to compromise, for we don't always know the right answers.

My platform will be based on strength and equality. Strong borders. We're a nation of immigrants, and we want them, but we want them under our terms, done legally, and we won't tolerate any disrespect for those criminally crossing our borders. We want people of all colors, religions, and sexual orientations to live without fear and to move up in society, but moving up depends on you. And we will have the best services for our military veterans. It is high time that any American who served our nation honorably should not have to die or go hungry because they weren't given the proper treatment. We owe them that, and if there needs to be a complete overhaul of our Veteran's Administration, and a change in how we finally support other nations, then by God, we will do it. That garnished some more applause. It's easy for a President, or candidate, to make these promises, but it takes a Congress to make them law.

And we're a progressive country. We're a country of great ideas and inventions, and nothing should ever stop that progress, but the way the American people accept new products and ideas must come from the American people, not forced down their throats. Many factors come into play when advancing an industry, such as cost and implementation. We can remain energy independent and yes, still find new sources of oil, while preparing for the next generation of energy. More applause. Somebody yelled "Dig, baby, Dig". Milt wouldn't utter those words, but if digging was required to keep oil flowing at market prices, he certainly wouldn't sign an Executive Order stopping it. He believed that one day, there would be better alternatives to oil, and several were showing promise, but the switch couldn't be made overnight. It never is.

The speech ended and the crowd dispersed. Within an hour, the media responded. The left attacked him as the same old racist, narrow-minded thinking from previous candidates. They even projected he was "not a candidate to be concerned about, because he would not satisfy the rabid hunger of the far right, and not provide progressives with the answers they want, either. With that, they might not have been far off the mark.

A conservative media outlet wrote. "In reading between the lines of Governor Greenbaum's speech, we can see some of what we've seen in Georgia for over seven years, a weakening of conservative principles in the name of 'unity'. You can expect, with a President Greenbaum, some victories, and many defeats, as his "reach across the aisle" results in a further erosion of our Republican values. Others were more conciliatory, even one saying, "Finally, common sense. Governor Greenbaum will help stop the divide between parties and work to reach middle ground, to act in a spirit of common sense." But did the people want compromise? Did they want common sense?"

Getting his team together would be hard work, but long before Milt made his announcement, he had obtained the services of Dan Bennett, a seasoned political manager who had national experience working on Presidential campaigns. He also went way back with Milt, as they were in the same law school class at Emory. It would prove to be much different than his gubernatorial campaign. For Georgia, Greenbaum conceded many points and mostly stuck to a Republican platform after seeing that he could win that way. But with a commitment not to spend more than 25% of his sizable fortune on this new venture, he relaxed. In his lifetime, he dreamed of going out and speaking about what he believed was "his truth", words he detested. The truth was the truth, and opinion was opinion.

Nobody would be spared criticism during a Greenbaum candidacy, and he was preparing himself for the fireworks. He decided to start a book nearly 18 months prior to his announcement, and with Dan's help, it would go out in another week. Advance copies were sent out by his publisher, and already, he had many requests for interviews.

# Common Sense

**Excerpt from the new political book "Milt Greenbaum: Common Sense."**

**INTRODUCTION:**

*Hello. My name is Milton Greenbaum. Please, call me Milt. My friends do. I have found Milton to be very formal. Like my mom was calling me from downstairs, "Milton, get downstairs right away." Oh-oh. So, I gravitated to Milt. Of course, as I grew up and entered the professional ranks of life, I was called many things. Let's start with the good titles. There was Milt Greenbaum, Linebacker, University of Memphis Tigers. Well, that's not a title, but I love college football to this day, and I loved being a Tiger. Okay, we weren't the Crimson Tide, but we had a darn good football team. Well, don't look at 1989, or '87, but we WERE 6-5 in 1988 and beat the #14 ranked team, the Florida Gators. Okay, those weren't our glory years, and no, I didn't get drafted, but I learned a lot. Mostly, to find another occupation. But seriously, I looked mean enough, from all those hours in the weightroom, but I was too slow for big-time college or pro football. Fortunately, my parents instilled in me the motivation (or the fear) to study hard, and my grades got me into the Emory School of Law. I was always intrigued by the law. I like orderly things, but in law, it was more than that. It was using the law to your advantage, it was careful questioning, detective work, and sometimes, well, often making deals. I loved it all.*

*So, one thing, or conversation, led to another, and I discovered a career in the Judge Advocate General Corps. I had a new title, Lieutenant Greenbaum. By the time I was done, twelve years later, I was Major Greenbaum. I left the Army and became an attorney, in private practice, in Atlanta, GA. By now, I was married, had a wife, Debbie, a daughter, Bev, and a son, Adam. Life was great and always getting better.*

*Maybe you're heard of Greenbaum's Grocery Stores? Of course, if you grew up in northwestern Mississippi, or around Memphis or Louisville, you have. We were quite large, and it goes all the way back to the early 1900's, when my great-grandfather, Isidore Greenbaum, moved here from Russia. A farmer, he sort of stumbled across the concept of starting a market. Many of the Jewish people from Clarksdale, the town that welcomed our family, were shop keepers of some kind. So, from there, it started. One little store in Clarksdale, then a second, and then every year it seemed, a few more. By the time my dad took over, we were, I suppose you can say, a regional powerhouse, with TV commercials, jingles, and all of that. Certainly, you must remember the catchy tune, "Greenbaum's, Greenbaum's, Fresh Groceries with a Smile." We also had what we called our "Road Series" commercials. Yup, I was in them, in the car, yelling 'are we there yet?'. Always smiling people, picnics, lots of fresh food, and the closing slogan at that time, "Greenbaum's, Greenbaum's, Fresh Service with a Smile....mile after mile." After my great granddad, whom I never met, was my grandfather, Benjamin, or "Bennie" Greenbaum and of course, my dad, Robert, "Robbie" Greenbaum. You see, none of them liked formal names. My dad and grandpa always walked the aisle, talking to customers, trying to help those in need. My Great Grandad knew every customer by name in Clarksdale, but of course, that became impossible for the next two generations, but we were grateful. I was taught that everyone was the same, a person of value.*

*Born in 1967, I never saw the Jim Crow existence for Black people in the South, buy my dad saw plenty. There wasn't a whole lot our family could say publicly, according to my dad. We had a business and a growing number of employees who depended on us for their livelihood. What we could do, they would say, is keep making business prosper, hire people of all colors and backgrounds, and be good citizens. "Change will eventually come", they would say, and change has most certainly come, even if many people believe that more still needs to happen.*

*Greenbaum is a Jewish name, and my family participated in the Jewish community of both Clarksdale and Memphis. My Great-Grandpa was one of the founders, in 1910, of the first synagogue in Clarksdale, and then in 1929, when they moved to a larger building on Catalpa Street. We were never terribly religious but observed major holidays. I rolled my eyes, then, and a little now, at how ignorant people would make assumptions on who Jews were, often from seeing the ultra-religious and their attire, and culture. I mean, I'm a Tennessee boy, right where the borders of TN, MS, and Arkansas came together, with the mighty Mississippi River flowing right next to downtown Memphis, next to Beale Street, where Louis Armstrong, Muddy Waters, Roscoe Gordon, and B.B. King once entertained and enthralled. I moved to Memphis when I was three. I adopted a love of football, BBQ brisket, the blues, and boiled peanuts. I watched MASH and Bugs Bunny. We had no secret meetings in the basement, and we didn't drink anybody's blood. I'd say, we were sufficiently boring and not much different than the many non-Jewish friends I had. Still, when people are different, there are questions, and sometimes, suspicions. That's why openness, listening, and kindness goes a long way. Smiling helps, too. Besides, the last people who will want to convert you are Jews. As Archie Bunker said about that in "All in the Family", one of my top five TV shows of all time, "They don't won't ya!". Ha! If I become President, nobody has to worry about my religion one way or another. I've told you who I am, and I have no secrets. It's probably the least important part of why you would, or wouldn't vote for me, but people will wonder, and people will ask questions. Okay, go ahead and ask. I just don't think it's too important. You folks just go on being whatever religion you want to be, or none. I won't make decisions based on my religion. I don't even know what those decisions would be if I wanted to do that? Don't eat pork? Umm, ever hear of Rendezvous, or Interstate, or Corkey's BBQ? Or near my current home in Atlanta, Fox Brothers or Heirloom? My goodness. If you know me, and maybe you'll have a good idea soon, I love my BBQ.*

*One of the hardest decisions I ever made in my life was to walk away from the family grocery business. I was a 4th generation Greenbaum, and it meant a lot. But my father, Robert "Robbie" Greenbaum, stressed to always follow my own dreams. That dream was to enter the military and study law, so after my days at the University of Memphis, I headed one state over to Georgia, and got a law degree at Emory. Hey, where did the Southerners go? I met people from all over at Emory and got an excellent education that prepared me for the Georgia Bar. That's what I needed to join the Army's JAG program for the next several years, and I eventually earned a new title, Major. I can't tell you how rewarding my twelve years in the United States Army was. I was stationed all over, in the U.S., and some of that time in Germany.*

*I met my wife Debbie through mutual friends while I was stationed at Fort Stewart, in Georgia, and Debbie was living in Savannah. We met at a religious service there, which surprised me, because that wasn't something I gave much thought to, but it did get me back to my roots a little bit. So, just 18 months later, I married the former Deborah Grossman. I guess "when you know, you know". Just a year later, our daughter Beverly was born. We call her Bev, and then two years later, Adam was born. I had passed ten years of service, and Deb and I started talking about our future. I suppose we did that before we were married, but it was nearing the time for me to leave the Army, as it wouldn't be long before I turned the big 4-0. I made it a point to begin looking for the right practice. I kept my Emory and Atlanta connections, and eventually, I took a job as an attorney with a firm in Atlanta. Deb wanted to put down roots and stay in one city for a while. She was a University of Georgia graduate, so she was happy to be only 90 minutes away from the Athens campus. Throughout our home you can find the occasional drawing or stuffed tiger or bulldog.*

*I had given thought to one day leaving the legal profession, and maybe trying my luck in the political arena. I got very active in Atlanta-area service organizations, something the Greenbaum family did a lot of through the family grocery chain. Naturally, I worked there continuously, part time, until I left for law school. I never really considered myself as Governor, but things have a way of falling into place sometimes.*

*I think being a Governor is a great prerequisite for becoming a President, though it has only been a recent occurrence for me to contemplate running for the Presidency. Large corporations often want somebody to "work up from the bottom". You know, the mailroom, or an entry-level salesperson, then a Regional Manager, maybe a stint at one of the overseas divisions. Shouldn't it be the same for the Presidency? The most important job our nation has? Certainly, being a Governor means you have a budget, you preside over the national guard, a legislature, and work with foreign governments. And then, with so much money going to the military, and the complexity of it, shouldn't the President understand how the military works? Well, here I am, Governor, and I was an Army Major. That' s a pretty good resume, if I say so myself. I think I'm ready for the next step.*

*The fact is, I don't like the way the country is changing. I have always felt that at the end of the day, WE are responsible for our lives. The Constitution is a wonderful document that gives us the freedom to pursue our dreams. It's not the Constitution that has sometimes held us back, but a divided, bigoted, nation. Perhaps it's the people themselves.*

*I love our freedom so much that I am very open to different ideas, and the fact that people have different opinions. The problem with our nation today is that politicians believe they can only win by taking a partisan position. They are either totally in the Democratic camp, or totally in the Republican camp. You might not ever know how they feel, because every day, they check and see which way the wind is blowing. But you can't blame them entirely, because isn't that what YOU, the public wants?*

*I told myself that if I was ever in the financial position to run a campaign and tell the public how I really felt, then gosh-darn it, I might just do it (don't worry, I don't really speak that way, and if you heard me when I stubbed my toe at 3:00 AM, on the way back from the bathroom, you'd know it!).*

*So, who am I? Well, you'll find out in these pages, but I believe in complete transparency. In today's age, 2024, society would consider me a conservative Republican, so immediately, half the country hates me, I suppose. BUT WAIT!! Not so fast. We must talk. I won't make everyone happy. That's impossible, but I'm going to speak honestly and politely. Believe it or not, you won't hear me blasting my opponents, calling them idiots, or anything like that. Don't believe me? Well, you'll find out. If we want a more polite society, it needs to start with our leaders. But I will disagree with people, politely, but firmly.*

*You are likely to see me be a little bit more liberal (which is not a bad word, conservatives) on social issues, to a point, of course, and more to the right on fiscal issues. The Libertarians will try to claim me, and I'm glad to have them. I'm a Capitalist. Sorry to those with the "Che" t-shirts, but I believe in it. That doesn't mean we don't have some social services, but we need people out there competing hard, learning, getting better, making more money. We need strong borders. What? We're not allowed to have that, but other countries can. Of course, we want immigrants. That's who we are, but we need a system we can control. Doesn't that just make sense?*

*Nothing is free. Let's remember that. We can scream about all the free things we want. We can march, block roads, go onto talk shows. All those things, but it won't change this fact. In the end, somebody pays. We can compromise. We can consider policies and programs to delay payments, to reduce payments, to help train people, but everybody needs to have some skin in the game. That's how I was raised, and I believe in it.*

*I was also raised to believe in the individual. Several minorities in the country were treated terribly. There is no place for racial injustice, or discrimination based on religion, race, sexual orientation, or national heritage, but we can't take revenge on others for the actions of their ancestors. How does that promote equality? Of course, it doesn't. We can't change the past, but in my life, and in a Greenbaum Presidency (wow, sounds great), people will be judged on their individual merit. Just like a quote from one of my favorite movies, "How Green was my Valley", "You cannot fight injustice with more injustice. Only with justice." See the movie. It's a good one.  Maureen O'Hara was a beauty.*

*I thought long and hard about running for the Presidency. I'm taking a "Common Sense" approach. My views, and I won't alter them without listening long and hard. We're allowed to change our mind, but in most key areas, my mind is probably set. It was honed during the many dinners with my parents and grandparents. They learned about hard work and being gracious in Clarksdale, MS.  Treat people the way you wish to be treated. Not so hard, really, and the good news? Every major religion has a version of "The Golden Rule". Use it. It will rarely fail you, but if you must disagree, then attack ideas, not the person expressing them. It can be done.*

*You won't like everything I have to say. I'm going to be critical of just about everyone, and you'll be critical right back. That's fine. If you like what I have to say, vote for me. If not, well, then don't. I don't need the money. Is that arrogant? I hope not, but I want you to know that I don't feel obligated to lie to anyone. That's a rarity in politics, perhaps, but it isn't at all rare for me. I believe in personal responsibility, and if you believe somebody else is more responsible for your decisions than you, well, then I guess we'll butt heads. As a former linebacker, I was pretty good at butting heads, and I'll win most of those battles, but that doesn't solve many problems.*

*You can disagree, even firmly, without screaming profanities, even when you're not online. Boy, the internet is a paradox, isn't it? So great for information, for meeting old friends, for knowledge and entertainment, that is, when it's not a cesspool of rudeness. But that's freedom. Sometimes, we must pay for our freedom in blood. Other times, through "trolls".  Freedom isn't free.*

*I'll never forget the time people were online, arguing the merits of Capitalism vs. Socialism. I decided to solve the problem, while at the same time, make peace and be an internet hero. So, I wrote, "I believe that Capitalism has been the best method of lifting people out of poverty and enriching a country. However, we need government, we need some programs to help people, and we need to fight greed regardless of what system we are under." I thought, "not bad". Well, I was wrong. Somebody thought it WAS bad, because their response to me was, "Please do us all a favor and kill yourself." Wow, the internet folks!* 😊

*Read the book, please. Stick with it. We'll address all the key issues, and yes, I have opinions. I believe in what I believe. Some of it, you've heard. Sometimes, I use my gut. I believe in nature, in order, that so much of our success and failure begins at home, so I believe in strong, whole families, and in loving discipline. Is that the only way? No, of course not. But it's best. I believe everybody has the right to life, meaning I just lost half of you again, but don't act prematurely. You haven't heard the entire story.*

*Let's get back to some common sense for this country. That begins by listening, by expressing our opinions without a nasty comment. Look, life is hard. Arguments can get heated. I get that, and I won't shy away from it. But we can all use a little more "Golden Rule" in our lives, including the President.  It's just common sense."*

Dan arranged for the introduction to be offered free online. He began making videos. All had a common thread, a common theme, and that theme was "common sense". It was done as a "man on the street type of interview." Milt Greenbaum was a nice guy, but a guy not afraid to say the "the king has no clothes", without tearing somebody down. He believed in personal responsibility and the Constitution. It wasn't necessary for everybody to believe in the same things, or to even get along all the time. It was necessary to tell the truth, to listen, be willing to compromise, to expect and reward results, and that started with our leaders.

# The National Interview

CNN came calling, which was located right down the road in downtown Atlanta. He agreed to a 30-minute interview special. "The Presidential Candidacy of Georgia Republican Governor Milton Greenbaum." Already, Milt didn't like it. "Republican", he asked Dan. "Well, you didn't think you'd escape that, did you?" was Dan's response. "Well, half of America already hates me, and most of them probably won't even watch." "Milt", Dan said. "You're going to face the same scrutiny as any candidate. Assumptions will be made strictly on your party affiliation. The worst assumptions. You're meeting America, and first impressions count. You are your own man. Party affiliation is important, but you make your own decisions. You did it in the Army; and you did it as a Governor. You weigh all options. You let the facts come out. You listen to people on both sides. You always listen. That's important. You don't make assumptions. You wait for the facts. You consider all sides. I'm not telling you what to say or how to think. If I didn't know your record already and believed in you, I wouldn't work for you. It's that simple. You're a seasoned lawyer. You were born for this, or rather, trained for this." "For what?" asked Milt. "For people to try and throw you off your game, trick you, get you to say something you didn't really mean? Anything to make you look bad?" "The media people who lean left, and that's a lot of 'em, Milt, will break out of the gates and try to hurt your campaign, and the few that lean right are going to be skeptical that you're not a RINO ("Republican in name-only"). Worst of all, you can't appear to be weak. Wishy-washy." Milton said, "Dan, I've thought about this for a long time. The lies, the hypocrisy, and the nastiness. I'll be forthcoming, honest, and I realize that means that everyone will find something not to like about me." "Well,", Dan said. Don't go halfway. You're not the only one who has wondered if there were any more honest politicians left. I'm not sure, Milt, that this is a winnable campaign under that strategy, but it's an honest one," and they both chuckled, but only slightly. It was going to be rough.

The CNN anchor began by introducing Milt as if nobody knew him, and really, how much would anyone expect a resident of Idaho or even New York or California, to know about the Governor of Georgia, so they began with a background of Dan's birth in Clarksdale, his family's legacy with the Greenbaum's grocery chain (also unknown to most outside of the chain's marketing area), a slight nod to his Jewish faith and what that would mean for Americans, and of course, a discussion of the key issues, like the economy, education, national security, energy, healthcare.

The drama with Milt Greenbaum didn't really come from all the main issues of the day. On an economic front, Greenbaum had made a statement that the "Fair Tax" would be an interesting model to look at, and naturally, somebody dug it up, and he was asked about it. Milt was "prepared enough" to discuss a topic very few Americans would even understand, and that two institutes couldn't agree on it. Milt answered by saying, "I never said I agree with the Fair Tax because it has never been executed. Some say it would stimulate the economy. Others say that only the wealthy would benefit." The host chimed in, "But haven't you said that the wealthy has been punished for their success." "I said, 'at times. I don't like short cuts for anybody, and if you'd like, I can send you a couple dozen soundbites where I say that." I don't like individual or corporate loopholes, nor do I like wealthier individuals being taxed at a heavier rate, strictly because they earn more. However, they need to pay their fair share. That doesn't mean a higher rate, but this Fair Tax needs to be tested. First, let's devise a way to put it into practice before we restructure our entire economic system. So, it needs more research. I've said that before, and I'll say it here, and we have 30 minutes, now twenty minutes, so I don't know that we should take more time on it, but I'll return if you'd like, and we'll get some economic experts on both sides.

But here's what I will say about taxes, and like my book, let's try to be practical about it. Number one, we need taxes. We can debate social programs later, but what is a social program? Are roads, the military, public schools, Medicaid, social programs? Of course. There are programs for the general benefit of society. But everybody should be paying taxes. There's the never-ending discussion of how much? Should the rich pay more because they can? Well, when we say "more", we're talking, usually, about a higher rate. I will tell you something radical you're not hearing anywhere else. I tend to be against tax breaks for anybody. You earn an income, you pay taxes. I would do away with mortgage interest tax, most deductions, in general. But if you're wealthy, you would be incentivized to earn more to pay a lower rate." "The rich pay a lower rate?" "Don't some pay none? Isn't that what many people argue?" "Yes," the reporter said, "We do see that. "Well," Milt said, "Have you heard of volume buying? If you buy more, you get an overall discount. "If you make $1 million, your rate goes down, but you don't get the usual tax breaks. The government will get more money than before, and people have an inventive to earn more." On the other end, yes, Americans under a certain annual income would pay nothing. Living for them and affording housing, groceries, and so forth, is difficult enough, but the middle class would pay a certain amount and have very few instances of being able to deduct. No hiding, any longer. I would remove the standard and itemized deductions. If you lose money, well, better luck next time. That loss, of course, lessens your tax burden as far as that goes, but I don't consider that a deduction. Taxes would normally be owed on your adjusted gross income, but there would be few adjustments to make. We can try the Fair Tax, as I've said, if it could be measured in a real-life situation. People cannot cry at "the rich" getting away with murder any longer, but if they perform, they get an incentive. That's the American way. But they aren't allowed to do what some people call cheating, even if the current tax code allows it.

They moved on.

They talked about social issues, which is what the country spent most time discussing, anyway. "Do you think America is a racist country." "Well," Milt responded, "the way that word is used, misused, and tossed around, if I said no, then people would be screaming that I hate Black people, or other non-white people. Instead, let me answer it my way, and I think you'll get your answer. This country has a history of bigotry against many groups. None has compared to the plight of Black people. You can't put language, words, to slavery, keeping people in chains, and the fact that many prominent Founding Fathers kept slaves means, to me, that they were racist, that they thought Black people were fundamentally less intelligent than white people. Well, that's simply not true. That doesn't mean you tear down statues of Founding Fathers who did much good, either. Black people have proven, time and again, that they can be prominent in any field, from math, to science, to engineering, to the athletic and artistic fields. We've come a long way. Is there institutional racism? Laws, such as the Jim Crow laws, we had here in the South. No, I don't see them, so I would say we no longer have "Institutional Racism", or "systemic racism", that would be, state-sponsored racism. It would have to be pointed out to me. But we have division, we have bigotry, prejudice. We have people that do not like a person because of the color of their skin, or their religion, or their sexual preference. It's wrong, but the government can only do so much. Hate is taught, like acceptance and kindness. I learned most of that at home. It was taught to me, and when I say that I'm referring to acceptance, tolerance, and kindness. Not hate. But let me talk about the other side of the coin. I use the expression quite a bit, that says, 'For you cannot fight justice with more injustice. Only with justice.' That comes from a great movie, by the way, called "How Green was my Valley", about the lives of Welsh Coal Miners. I highly recommend it." Milt tried his hand at being human for a moment. "I would like our nation to do what it can to defeat bigotry, and yes, racism. Let's not think that punishing people today who had no part in racism is the answer to our problems." The reporter said. "Well, what are some examples of that?" Milt answered. "Separate graduation ceremonies and organizations, affirmative action, the entertainment industry establishing quotas. Instead, dedicate yourself to using merit as an indicator, and ignoring race. Do people want bigotry and racism to go away, or do they simply want to target another group, perhaps the former perpetrators? Then that goes on for fifty years until that group somehow gets their power back. Where is the end? The government is not, and should not be, the final word. I don't want to tell Black Lawyers that they can't have an association of Black Lawyers. That's not the government's job. But what I AM saying is, "let's learn from our mistakes as a nation and move forward without making the same mistakes again." The CNN reporter seemed dissatisfied and said, "Many people believe these programs are the only way to give African Americans and people of color an opportunity, a level playing field." "I don't agree", said Milt. They have proven themselves many times over, and like all persecuted minorities, they need to dedicate themselves to outperforming society as a whole. That is the only way to catch-up, or at least the best way." "A lot of people will come away believing that you don't want to help African Americans." "Well, that's the opposite of the truth. I can cite many reasons of how I have lived by example, but in the end, there are no shortcuts. Just leave Black people alone, is what I would say. Treat them with complete equality, which we don't always do, but we need to do that, and they also, like any group, must do better. Educate themselves, articulate better, present themselves better, keep their families together and obey the law. Many have done just that and thrived. Fifty years ago, Black people in the South could not eat at a luncheon counter. Now, we've had a Black President, CEOs, and Black people, by law, are not discriminated against. There may be bigotry, and we may still have a long way ago, and we must do better. White people must do better, and all people.

The reporter continued, as something was an annoyance to her. "I noticed you don't say 'African American'. Why not?" Because a Black friend told me that he thought it was disrespectful. It was as if they needed a special designation. He said, 'I've never even been to Africa. I'm an American, like you. Why isn't that good enough?' In the spirit of treating everybody the same, I call all citizens of this country Americans. To me, that's an honor. Don't you think so?" "Well," the reporter said, "We have so many problems in this country, I don't think you can call it great." "I'm sorry you feel that way. I understand what you're saying, but I don't agree with your opinion on that at all. This country has done some terrible things, but also great things, so I love being an American. We can do a lot of things better. I'd like to help, so we have that in common. We both agree that we can do better. Milt smiled, "and you know, I have a friend who was in born in Cape Town, South Africa, and moved here when she was 22. She's white, and she's an African American, more so than my Black friend, who has never been to Africa. Wouldn't you say so?" The CNN reporter gave him a smirk, and said, "Let's move on."

The CNN anchor continued. "Doesn't your overall racial and equality theory cast doubt on you as a person?" Milt didn't like it but answered it. "That I believe people should be judged on their own merit? I hope not. Look, this country has done terrible things to minorities in general, and to Black people in particular. The answer is to eliminate, by law, discrimination, and then, as much as I hate to say it, that group needs to outperform other groups simply to be looked upon as equal." "What does that mean?" the reporter asked. "Look at our Asian population. They were once treated poorly, and I don't mean to say that there isn't any anti-Asian sentiment today, but today, it is probably envy, because they decided, as a group, maybe not together, but consciously, to study and work hard, and today they are among the most successful minorities in America." "So, the reporter said, "You are willing to tell Black voters that the reason they suffer from racism is because it is their fault?" "I'm here to tell the truth", Milt said, "and the truth is that they've been treated in a way no group should be treated, and yet, now that the law is at least more on their side, that institutional racism is gone or lessened, that they will have to pull themselves up by their bootstraps, which many have done, which most can do, but it starts with them, just like I would tell any group." Milt continued, "You're an Atlanta resident, a Georgia resident. Would you like to review the members in my cabinet, or contracts I've awarded to black companies?" "No," said the reporter. "I've seen it". Milt said, "I've gone out of my way to give our Black community every opportunity, and the ones chosen for projects, I felt, were the most qualified. I've also said "no" to some companies because they weren't the most qualified, and that could mean that their quotes were too high. Look, we can't change the past, but we CAN be 100% fair moving forward, but that means that Black people will win some and lose some. Eventually, they will win more. Just leave them alone. Give them freedom. Treat them with the same dignity as everybody else. That's my belief and if some people believe that makes me racist, well, I've seen Black surgeons I would send my children to, God-forbid, if they were sick. I've seen Black musicians who are geniuses at their craft, Black CEO's. I respect them, I don't pity them, but they have challenges as well, naturally. Some are self-induced." "But" the reporter said", not a Greenbaum fan, and sensing a pivotal moment to cause injury, "You don't believe we live in a racist country, and that we have no systemic racism?" Milt took about five seconds, while the reporter arched his eyebrows. "I think this country has come a long way, and I'm proud of it. Black people can accomplish anything anybody else can accomplish. I don't deny that there's racism, but we no longer have the type of racism we once had. There are no longer laws that prevent Black people from living in freedom the way white people do. Is there prejudice? Well, naturally, there is prejudice in every shape and form imaginary, and it sickens me. People who simply don't like Black people, or Jewish people, or Asian people. We must squeeze out the remaining bigotry, or, if you want to call it racism, you may, but they're not the same thing. We must spend time together. Black people have all sorts of abilities, personalities, just like anybody else, and my experience with them is largely, very positive. I say that there are problems in the Black community, statistics that show too many families broken apart, like other groups, but higher, and our society is only strong when families are strong. Incarceration rates are too high. A feeling of hopelessness. As a society, we must listen, pay attention, assist, but in the end, Black people must do it themselves. There is no better time. I know they're in a hole, many are, and it's easy to feel despair and give up, turn to drugs, or crime. Again, they're not alone, but they have, by far, the highest rate of incarceration in the country.

There was no way there would be an interview with a Jewish candidate without mentioning Israel and the terrible problems in the Middle East, and the interviewer asked for an assessment."

"The short answer is, Israel is our strongest ally in the Middle East, and we will continue to support them. We do not exist in order to run another nation, including Israel. Let's not forget or response when America was attacked at Pearl Harbor. We defended our nation and responded with overwhelming force, once we reached Japan. That's war. Israel was brutally attacked in October of this past year, and they have every right to locate and destroy the terrorist group that attacked them so brutally.  I have, for reasons that should appear obvious, downplayed my religion and my feelings on the Middle East, but I also promised that my campaign would be one of total truth. The nation of Israel is a sovereign state, and they will remain so. I don't recall their people dancing in the streets after 9-11 like I saw the people in the West Bank and Gaza do. Let's not forget that.

A few more questions were asked, but the interview ended and many in the media would paint Milt Greenbaum as nothing more than a run of the mill Republican. Denying racism, not caring for the poor, when he honestly believed his message. He had no feelings of bigotry toward anyone. He just didn't think the past should be used to determine the future. It was time to move on. Easy for him to say? Well, many things are easy for him to say. He had rich parents and never wanted a thing, but it wasn't always that way in his family, and he believed everything he said.

The conservative press generally gave him good marks. Some said he could be more forceful, but in general, he hit on all the Republican talking points.

Other papers, talk shows, and bloggers picked up on the story. Naturally, the more humorous shows had to find ways to ridicule him. He was hit too many times playing football, and the Army finished the job. He was called "Republican Light", disliked by the left and not respected by the right, and yet, people were talking about him.

One network commentator had the guts to say that he "told the truth", whatever that was, but he was too right for the left, and not right enough to the right, leaving him in "no man's land". Sure enough, a political cartoonist drew him on a battlefield, complete with World War One era trenches, mud, barbed wire, stuck right in the middle. The title read, "Milt Greenbaum. "The Phantom Candidate". Well, Dan said, he just did Milt a big favor, by giving him a name. "Hey" he told Dan, "Press is press". Even bad news is news. The media will want you, and by the next day, he was getting a call from a major network, late night talk show, where he got a lukewarm reception. "Wow", said the guest, "It can take years for somebody to get a solid nickname, and you got one right out of the gate, "The Phantom Candidate!".

"So, Mr. Greenbaum, or do I call you Major Greenbaum or Governor Greenbaum." "You can call me Milt, if you'd like, or whatever you'd like." "Naw", the host smiled. "I wouldn't want to appear wishy-washy", prompting the audience to laugh out loud. Milt was warned very strongly by Dan not to take anything to heart, to laugh along. This was a big moment. His coming out party.

Milt smiled, then he said, "May I address that?" The host wanted to spend a minute properly introducing Dan to his national television audience. First, it was the humble Southern roots, first in Clarksdale, then Memphis, and the family grocery business." "So", the host continued, "you gave up a good job at the corner grocery store to become a lawyer?" Milt responded, "Yes", my dad sold the business, and I joined the Army. It was very rewarding." "Ok, ok" said the host, not exactly on Milt's side, but feeling he need to show at least a semblance of respect to a former Army Major and state Governor, even if it was Georgia.

"You know, I wanted to take two minutes to make my mark, and you can time me. It's now or never." Really? He turned to the band, a very cool eight-piece ensemble that played during all the beaks. Hey fellas, can you time him? How about playing something when he hits two minutes?" "Sure thing", said Sandy Blackman, the "Sandman", and they played a 4-second jingle that sounded like something played at the end of questioning for the dating game."

The show's host was being corny, but Milt was serious. "Ok, everyone, '3-2-1' and the audience followed along. Milt and Dan hoped the went right along. This part, at least, was part of the plan. Win or lose, he would get his message across." After "1", Milt began, and he stood, for effect.

"All my life, I've wanted to be President. It's one reason I joined the military and ran for Governor, where I served for eight years. I love this country, our freedoms, and our amazing document we call the Constitution. It's a great document, but we haven't always followed it. Even men with great ideas have done terrible things, enslaved others, kept others down and out, from enjoying equality, from basic rights. I can't argue these things. But eventually, through the bravery of many, we have improved, we have come a long way. We're not there yet but look at the progress we've made."

I believe in Capitalism. It is the single greatest means of lifting people out of poverty ever designed. If you don't agree, then I believe you haven't studied history and what Socialism has done to countries. But we still have some social programs. There is a balance, something we must look at one policy at a time. But without a sense of individualism, we won't have the means to help the less fortunate. Speaking of that, all Americans must take personal responsibility for their lives, their success. It is not for the government to prop you up. Everyone needs to have some skin in the game. If you borrow money, you've made a promise to pay it back. That's being an adult. We can discuss helping people, a helping hand, not a handout. We have to work together. Nobody wants to see people without medical care and homes, but those are commodities. People study and work to provide those things, so we need ways to provide basic care for people. Maybe if we gave less to other nations and kept that money at home, we'd be able to do more.

45-seconds left.

I believe in being strong militarily. We'll regret being weak and lose more lives that way. I believe that abortion should be legal, but life begins at conception. I hate the thought of abortion and I want to see programs to reduce it. I know it's controversial, there's no one-fix for all, but it's a death. Let's make it safe, legal and rare. People used to say that. Let's get back to it. We're a nation of immigrants but we can't simply open our borders up. Enough is enough. I'll secure the border and WE will decide who to let in. As much as I hate discrimination, you cannot fight injustice with more injustice. Eliminate special privileges based on race, sex, or national origin. Remember the

41

past but live for the future. Select and promote based on merit, and finally, treat people with more kindness and respect. My candidates might call me names, but I won't reciprocate. It's time for decency in politics, and it will begin with me".

Two seconds to spare.  Of course, the band got to play their little game show jingle, and the audience laughed. They also applauded Milt Greenbaum, mostly for finishing. Milt and Dan had that speech down to a solid two minutes and 26 seconds almost every time. That's why Milt asked for two and a half minutes. His speech would be scrutinized, and most definitely, disliked, by both sides. Oh my God, the right destroyed the abortion comment while the left gave it a "B", even if they didn't believe it. Really, there wasn't a comment that wasn't picked apart, but it was also brilliant in the minds of some. Milt was all the talk. He had a book, a CNN interview, and now, an interview on one of the leading talk shows. People saw him for what he was, a moderate conservative that was willing to reach across the aisle and consider reasonable compromise, but the question was, "did anybody really want that?".

# Back to Clarksdale

Milt was only three when his parents decided to move to Germantown, a nice suburb of Memphis, in 1970. They didn't want to do it, but it was necessary in order to run their business. Milt's Mom cried for days, but Robbie swore to her that the 80-mile distance wasn't so far that they couldn't go there regularly. That turned out to be an understatement. Besides, Robbie's semi-retired parents weren't going anywhere, and deliberately stayed in their modest home close to downtown, because it was "of bad character to shove our wealth down the throats of our neighbors." But who's kidding who? Once Greenbaum's opened its 50th store, the townspeople understood that the Greenbaum's were wealthy (if not long before that), so when Robbie and family moved away, an article appeared in the Press Register, explaining the departure of "one of Coahoma County's leading citizens". Except that it never really felt that way to many of their friends. The Greenbaum's never stopped supporting the synagogue, financially. They remained congregants even though they joined a place up in Memphis. How could they not, since Izzy was a founding member? Milt's Mom seemed to be there constantly, staying with the in-laws in town, playing Mah-Jong and stopping by at Abe's BBQ, usually bringing back a couple dozen "Big Abe's" pork and beef sandwiches, and ribs. She never stopped bragging to her Memphis friends that "Sure, Rendezvous is just fine, when you just must have BBQ, but don't begin to compare it to Abe's." Of course, everybody knew that both were excellent, but her Germantown and Memphis associates understood loyalty, and the Greenbaum's had it in spades. It was Clarksdale that allowed this family, their ancestors often persecuted; to settle in the deep south and gain a level of respect they couldn't attain anywhere else in the world. In America. In Mississippi. A local looked back today, in 2024, and said "Clarksdale back then was a 'mini-U.N.'" No grocery store, or seemingly ANY store, had more July 4th decorations adorning their stores as did Greenbaum's. The family also supported many a festival in Clarksdale, and many of the local churches, too.

It was a male bonding thing for the Greenbaum men to grab breakfast once a week at the Rest Haven, where Izzy first visited in 1947, their first year open. The very next week, he brought Bennie, who was thirty-four, and Robbie, who was twelve. But the greatest event, and there's a picture there to this day to prove it, was in 1967. Milt had just been born, and at eighty, Izzy was in failing health, so they hurried to the historic picture along. There they were, Izzy, Bennie, Robbie, and Milt, four generations of Greenbaum's, sitting down at the counter, Robbie holding a three-month old Milt. Naturally, there would be more photos taken, while they still had time, but Izzy said that the only thing better than sitting at Rest Haven with four generations of Greenbaum men, was having a slice of that amazing strawberry pie. Bennie said that the chocolate pie was better, and Robbie laughed and said, "Some things just aren't worth arguing about," and ordered a slice of each.

Not to play favorites, the Greenbaum clan could be seen at Ramon's and The Ranchero, for more great choices. It was at The Ranchero where Milt picked up his habit of pouring BBQ sauce into a bag of chips. He took that habit with him all the way to the Governor's mansion on West Paces Ferry in Atlanta. He laughed when he got stares. Not to be outdone was the Elite Cafe on Yazoo Ave downtown, and their famous "comeback sauce".  Of course, Milt was too young, but his dad, Robbie told him about going up to Conway Twitty's Moon Lake Resort, just a few miles up Friar's Point Road, for frog legs and catfish, and they had live music there Wednesday and the weekends. It took Milt awhile to figure out why Robbie, when feeling amorous, would walk up to his mom and sing,

Yes, while Milt grew up in Germantown, he was born in Clarksdale, and took that 80-mile drive so often, South on 61, through Tunica. Naturally it was nearly impossible to pass by the "Blue and White" restaurant on 61, without stopping, where every member of the family had eaten more times than they can count. It was a great stopping-off point, roughly halfway between Memphis and Clarksdale. From the homemade vegetable soup to the chicken livers with gravy that Milt couldn't get enough of, it just seemed like one item was better than the next. Milt joked that if there was a dictionary defining "Homecooked Southern Food", a photo of the Blue and White would naturally be there.

Milt was in Clarksdale so often that he usually just told people he was from the town, because the family's "soul" resided there. And if anybody wanted more proof, they would all eventually rest at the Beth Israel Cemetery, just north of town, also on Friar's Point Road.

Of course, Clarksdale was known as the "Birthplace of the Blues", and right next to Abe's BBQ was the famous "Crossroads" of highways 61 and 49, where legend had it that musician Robert Johnson sold his soul to the devil in order to become a great blues player. Muddy Waters and Sam Cooke would follow.  As a matter of fact, Robbie, only four years younger than Sam, brought him back to Clarksdale in 1961, as part of an anniversary celebration of Clarksdale, at the original store at the corner of DeSoto and North State Street. Hanging on the wall was a photo of Sam with the handwritten message, "To the Greenbaum Family, you Send Me".  That of course, referenced his top-selling song, written and recorded by Sam in 1957, and hitting number one on the Billboard Charts. Robbie was especially crushed when Sam was shot and killed in

December of 1964, in Los Angeles. In more recent times, Milt, a bona fide Blues fan (it was in his blood), would get back whenever he could through the years, to attend festivals and visit clubs in the area.

Milt  was more than a "native-born" Clarksdale person, it was his second home, and through his travels in the Army and around the world, he felt that even though he was a loyal "Red Devil" of Germantown High, where he was an all-state TN linebacker, his heart belonged to Clarksdale, the town that gave his family their first taste of freedom in America, and, like that strawberry pie at Rest Haven, it tasted awfully good.

# The Scene

Dan's phone rang off the hook, but that, of course, is a matter of speech. No more hooks, but his texts kept coming, social media kept talking about Milt, and Milt's phone kept ringing. A very popular woman's daytime talk show wanted Milt for the very next day, and Dan told Milt to "keep his schedule wide open for the next two weeks." So, Milt took a red eye from LAX to LaGuardia, to attend the 11:00 live version of "The Scene", an Emmy Award-winning show featuring a panel of very opinionated women, and they were either loved or despised by the viewing public. Dan walked in, in a navy blazer, sans tie, khaki pants. He got lukewarm applause, and one boo. Even the host, no friend of Milt's, reprimanded the one boo. "Now, now, we don't do that." Milt smiled. "Well, Governor Milt Greenbaum of Atlanta, Georgia, formerly from Memphis, Tennessee, formerly from Clarksdale, Mississippi. What's a nice Jewish boy doing from those kinds of places, and what's he doing running for President, of all things? I mean, you WERE a lawyer. Wasn't that good enough for your mom?" The audience laughed. The host worked on that half the night. After all, the ratings were predicted to be the highest they've had all year for Greenbaum, after that late-night show classic. "I know", laughed Milt. "I should at least be from the Bronx or Queens", setting off some laughter. "Don't be too funny", she continued, "You can't keep stealing everybody's thunder." More laughter, and Milt smiled. "Well,", Milt said, my family wanted me to take over the family's grocery business." "That's right", said the host. "Your family ran over 150 Greenbaum's grocery stores, all over the Memphis and Louisville areas, before selling to Kroger." "Yes", Milt said. "My great-grandfather, Isidore Greenbaum founded the business, and then my grandfather and father each took turns running it. But I decided to become a lawyer and enter the Army. It was a very tough, heart-wrenching decision, but family, as always, supported me, and I know that Kroger wanted to buy the chain, which certainly helped the family, financially." "Isn't it funny", the host said to no one in particular, "how people are so loyal to their grocery stores, but somebody on the other side of the country never heard of it? A friend of mine in Portland talked about growing up and always going to 'Fred Meyer'. I said, 'who'? She couldn't believe that I had never heard of Fred Meyer, but she never heard of Publix in Florida. It's funny how we're practically offended when somebody doesn't know 'our store'. There's HEB in Texas, Meijer in Michigan, Harris Teeter in North Carolina, Hannaford in New England." "And yet", said another panelist, "everybody has heard of Piggly Wiggly", and the audience laughed.

The criticism was coming. Milt knew it. They weren't on his side except for the one token Republican, and he wasn't so sure about her, either. "Actually", Milt said. Clarksdale, at one time, had a quite sizable Jewish population, and Memphis and Atlanta have vibrant Jewish communities."

"Well, in three minutes", one of the other ladies corrected her, "Two and a half". "Yes, yes, two and a half, you gave the world your entire state of the union the other night." "Well, no", said Milt, but people are tired of word salad, double-talk, phony comments. They want the truth, and they want answers, and you know, sometimes, 'I don't know' is an honest answer. Even acceptable"

The hosts spent nearly the entire hour dissecting his two (and a half) minute coming-out speech. They twisted it where they could, they baited him, but Milt had no problem weathering the storm. There were several instances of Milt saying, "I'm glad you asked that, and I'll explain exactly what I mean". They never seemed satisfied unless it was a comment that was generally in their favor, like abortion. "So", one of the more left-leaning members said, "abortion should be legal, period." "No, not period," said Milt, but I would compromise on this. Perhaps it's legal through the first trimester. Maybe it's a little longer, maybe it's five months. You do understand that for the strongest activists on both sides, either there are no limits, or it should be banned. That leaves no room for compromise. So, it is left to the states, and maybe that's the answer anyway. Some states will never ban it, and some already have, at least after a heartbeat is detected. I have already spoken my mind here. I don't want to see so many abortions, but I don't want the government making that decision for women, and in a country with so many feelings on this topic, I think most agree with me. Let's find ways to reduce it. To make it less necessary."

"You know", Milt continued. Too many people want their way. They're not interested in listening to reason, to common sense. They can't politely agree to disagree. They can't consider the other side, and people like me who have the guts to look you in the eye and tell you what I really think instead of what you want to hear, WE'RE labeled as cowards. I'm no coward. I've been speaking up against reverse discrimination. Don't tell me you hate how you've been treated and then applaud when people living with guilt propose policies that will enforce the same injustice, just not on you this time." Lo and behold, some in the audience applauded. "YES!" thought Dan, watching from the back of the stage. "I'll tell you something else. I don't need the power, and I don't need the money. I want to win. I think I CAN win, but if I lose, I won't have to worry about where my next meal is coming from. I've been very blessed. My family has done some wonderful things through several generations."

The moderator got a little testy, and things were about to boil over. "Are you saying that people who have been oppressed shouldn't be given opportunities to catch-up, that there shouldn't be a level playing field? Don't you think, as a white man, a person of privilege, you should step aside at times to give other people an opportunity." "Look, Wendy", Milt answered, doing all he could to keep his cool. "I believe in the equality of opportunity, not equality of outcome. Are you hosting this show because you have talent or is it because you're black?" "HOW DARE YOU!", came the response. She sat for a moment before hitting back, hard, "Well, maybe you're getting attention because you're a Jew, and nobody would give a damn about you if it wasn't for that. A Jewish Republican. An oddity." There was a loud moan from the audience. This WAS New York, after all, and a shaken Wendy said, "We're going to a commercial break."

Milt wanted to smile. Wendy was furious and the other ladies said nothing. In her earpiece, Wendy was being read the riot act. At one time she could be heard saying, "I don't care."

The eight commercials ended, and Wendy spoke first. "We're back on 'The Scene', with Presidential hopeful Governor Milt Greenbaum of Georgia, up to, perhaps, the same Republican tricks we've seen before. "Oh", asked Milt. "How so?" "I'm talking, Mr. Greenbaum". Milt laughed, gently nudging the lady beside him, and said, "I was Governor two minutes ago." "Well,", said Wendy, "Respect is earned, and this is my show. Our show." "Wendy, I respect you. You're an award-winning entertainer. I also knew most of you would ask me tough questions, be critical. You have to. It's the Presidency, after all. I do not believe in quotas or the affirmative action policies that I'm seeing more of. The motion picture industry is now interested in diversity more than choosing the best movie. I think you were chosen to moderate this show because you have talent and you're interesting. You've been successful in the business for a long time. You've earned it. Everybody should earn it. The President is decided by a vote. If American voters cast more votes for me, and I receive the Electoral Votes, then I will be President. You got angry at me for daring to think you may have gotten your job because you're black. Of course, I don't think that, and nobody should have to feel that way. That's why affirmative action is wrong, and I rest my case. Choose the best person for the job. Your network believes you earned it, and so you have. I'd hate for us to part ways angry, so please understand that I have tremendous respect for you. I respect all of you ladies. You have a tremendous show. You got high ratings and coming to this show was a great opportunity for me, and I thank you for it. We don't have to agree on everything, or even ANYTHING, to be civil, and I've tried to do that."

It was a slam dunk for Milt. He kept his cool, said his peace, and made the host of the show look foolish. In Dan's eyes, which was acceptable, too.

That night, Milt took an Uber over to Westfield, NJ, a very nice town in Union County, NJ, with a quaint, upscale downtown, and there, met Doctor Stan Wasserman, now Congressman in New Jersey's 11th Congressional District, a sort of oddly shaped area that started as a point around Westfield, and quickly moved to encompass a large swathe of rural western NJ all the way to Philipsburg and the Delaware River, and up to the mountainous northwest. Stan was a Democrat and former orthopedic surgeon whom Milt met in the Army. They were good friends, who despite their political differences, got along famously. They could be honest, joke around, even criticize and belittle, because each respected each other, and didn't let differences get in the way. In many ways, their political opinions were close to each other. They tended to sit close to the center, so where they differed was largely a matter of how involved the government might get in a policy or situation. Stan tended to invite more government participation, and Milt, less. But, depending on the subject, they could at least speak to each other. Of course, it wasn't all politics, either. It was sports, business, family. They were both Jewish, and that simply added another topic. Holiday plans, perhaps Israel, but neither wore their "Jewishness" on their shoulder, but neither would do anything to deny or dismiss it, either. It's what they were. It didn't define them, but when the time was right, or when it mattered, they cared about Jewish causes. Why shouldn't they? But even on that, it didn't mean that they were always on the same page.

"There he is the candidate." shouted Stan. "Shh" smiled Milt, as he extended his hand. "What's this hand, shit", said Stan, and wrapped Milt up in a bear hug. "Still got those meat hook arms, I see," said Stan. "Well, maybe, but I'm trying to thicken up the rest of my skin. I'm already taking a beating." "Well," you're out there in 'no man's land', my friend. Just a few little tweaks and we could get you to make the switch onto our team. There's still time! Imagine that speech!" "Ain't gonna happen, my friend. I'm still leaning right, to the good side." "Yeah, yeah," said Stan. "We can talk about it. I'll change your mind."

"Nah", said Milt. "Your side has drifted too far". We can at least discuss it. See where we can meet, but I knew going in that the country seems pretty black and white right now. You and I both know that what we want versus what the country thinks they want are two different things." "Well,", Stan said. "We've got a lot to undo. Sins of the past. When change is the right thing to do, Milt, there is no compromise." "Yes, but people can disagree over what's the right thing to do. It's not about somebody being 100% correct." "Well,", said Stan. "I already know the squirrel story". Both laughed. "It's way too simplified, Milt". "Yes, it's simple, but it's still on the mark. We need a government, we need ways to help the less fortunate, but at what point does the nation topple over, when we have too many in need and not enough to supply help? What if nobody gathers the acorns, my friend?" "I said no squirrels." Milt pointed to the menu. "Hey, this place has a squirrel entry. Did you bring it back from one of those western outposts of yours, like Harmony, NJ?" "Harmony is beautiful", Stan answered. "We're not called the 'Garden State', for nothing", answered Stan. You've got your peanuts and peaches, and we've got our tomatoes, corn, and cranberries." "Yeah, yeah," Milt smiled. "And Taylor Ham", said Milt. "Never heard of it", replied Stan, "Oh, maybe you mean pork roll", the two referencing the ages-old debate on what to call the timeless New Jersey meat delicacy, labeled pork roll, but once upon a time, 'Taylor Ham', though it was really pork all along. "Hey", said Stan, "as long as it's on a New Jersey hard roll with egg and cheese". "Yes", good stuff, agreed Milt. Politicians were known for knowing all the local cuisines, at least the one running for national office.

"So, you're up to your neck in it, but now you're known. You, my friend, have been on 'The Scene'". "Yup, I made it out of there alive." "Well, they're not worried about you. I'm afraid that the country knows what it wants. It's just that they don't want the same thing." "Stan, what I'm doing is right, at least for me. You know my stance. It's give and take. It's a blend. It's compassionate Capitalism, but it's Capitalism first. Why is it that most of the best ideas come from America, AND we give the most charity? Both! Both, my friend. Keep taking away individual initiatives, and give the government more power, then nobody will even feel like getting up in the morning. We can't raise the debt ceiling forever, my friend." "Can't we?" Stan replied, and both laughed. "Regarding that ceiling, it takes two to tango." "I know, I know," responded Milt. "Think I'm a dyed in the wool Republican?". "Well,", Stan replied, "to them, you're now forever a 'RINO'". "Yeah, don't I know it, but I knew that going in, and I'm sticking to my guns." "Milt, that's the problem", Stan said. "People are convinced that by being squarely in the middle, ok, a slight lean to the right," that you don't stand for anything." "That's B.S., said Milt. "I'm honest. If we make it more advantageous for people to slack off, they'll do it when they see that they won't be rewarded for getting ahead. Nobody said that we shouldn't have a safety net. It's quite simple, if you're down and out, get that temporary help and get back on your feet. It's not meant to be a forever thing. We need to place the emphasis on hard work and personal accountability. Make your riches, then give back what you can." "It sounds good up on a podium", replied Stan, but when corporations and the 1% are paying next to nothing, we can't even help those that desire to get back up on their feet, which, Milt, are most people." "But Stan", we're on the same side. We have to collect taxes. Let's re-do the tax code, even look at the

'Fair Tax'. Let's close the loopholes, but the rich shouldn't be paying at a higher rate. As a matter of fact, I propose we lower their rate. If they can hit an AGI of $1 million, lower that rate. Give them something to honestly shoot for."

"Lower the rate for the 1%", mocked Stand. "Good luck with that one."

"Look, Stan" said Milt with a smile. "You know me. You fixed my rotator cuff. You were in private practice, and you have nice things. Things you worked hard for. Graduated from Michigan Medicine." "I remember", said Stan. "Milt, it takes more than a warm handshake and promise to be nice. It takes the courage to fight for what you believe in. This country has made a lot of mistakes, and we have the means to get the homeless off the street, to feed people, to welcome more immigrants, to provide free healthcare. Much more." "Stan, I want to have a nice meal, not spend the next two hours arguing policy with you. You know my stance. I want to give Americans the freedom to help themselves, not to have the government do it for them. The Government hasn't done that correctly anywhere. We've got a good track record of the wealthy helping to feed people, help hospitals, invent life-changing products, and making this nation the best in the world. Let's keep that going or get back to it. There's corruption in the private sector and we know it's also in government, so force people to compete and make sure they don't cheat. Let's try to make more people rich. I have confidence in our people, Stan. They will give. We still need the government. We will need taxes, and we still need a safety net, but not at the risk of killing individual initiative." I trust people more than I trust the government. This is why we sit down and discuss, with passion. I can fight against you on policy, without calling you chunky, or hitting you." "Chunky?" said Stan, feigning hurt. It's true, Stan could spare to lose a few pounds". "That cuts deep", Stan said, knowing that Milt was a big "Andy Griffith Show" fan. "Deep", he said again, as Sheriff Taylor did.

"You know, I can't publicly endorse you", Stan said. "Of course, not", answered Milt. "And I'm going to be asked." "I know," said Milt. "Just say, well, he's obviously the best choice, but as a Democrat, I have to support my own party, even if they suck." "Yeah", laughed Stan, "That'll help my reelection efforts." "But you would if you could, right?" "No", said a serious Stan. I can work with you, but your ideas don't go far enough. If you win, I will support you, but, naturally, this is business." "Well, then you pay the check." "Stan", joked Milt, "When I win, we'll serve Taylor Ham in the White House." Stan rolled his eyes and said "There's no such thing. How can you be President when you can't read?". This was a reference, once again, to the popular NJ breakfast meat, made in in NJ, which was initially called ham and many years ago, was forced to change the name to pork, which is what it really is. But some northern Jersey folks insist on calling it Taylor Ham. Just one of many subjects that Jerseyans like to argue about. Milt was a TN and GA boy but knew Stan like a book.

"Well, Milt, what's next?" "I take my message to the people. I'll tell them how I think. I might be booed but I won't hold anything back. People will know where I stand unless I'm undecided. Some topics don't have easy answers," said Milt. "But, Milt, as a friend, I'm telling you, don't come off as a softie, even if those arms of yours can put a dent in the Washington Monument. I'll be asked about you and I'll do my best, but I can't support you, not in public, anyway." With the meal over, Milt notified Uber to return for him. He had a flight in the morning.

# On Tour

Milt stayed busy. He went back to California and spoke to a large, politically powerful group of gays and lesbians in San Francisco. While many would never vote for him, they had a tough time poking holes in his platform, at least about gay and lesbian issues. Yes, he supported gays and lesbians. Georgia had previously banned same-sex marriage until the passing of Obergefell v. Hodges, making the procedure legal in all fifty states. Milt said he would have passed it anyway, but it passed one year before he became Governor. The audience groaned as if to say, "we don't believe you", but he said, "if two consenting adults of the same sex want to get married, that is their private affair. It is legal and it is behind us now." I have always felt that being gay didn't mean that you didn't have concerns about taxes, business, national defense, and that you all felt the same on every topic.

"Let me start as I usually try to do. I'm a big believer in beginning at a high level. Some use the phrase, "10,000 feet". Basic thoughts. Not because you can't understand highly detailed ones, but because it removes some of the misunderstanding." Then, we "drill down", another business term, and figure out what we want to discuss. Some people think, when I or others do this, it's a "dumbing down", or I'm insulting your intelligence, but I'm not." The audience said nothing. No reaction.

I am running for President. That is an administrative job. It is not a religious job, it does not dictate moral conviction, nor actions beyond what is in the U.S. Constitution. It is my job to protect what you find in that document. When a President takes an oath, well, that's the oath. They swear to protect that document. Now we know, in real life, people want to know the President's, or candidate's views on many different topics. This is an organization of people who happen to be gay. If I had tried to form policy that in one way or another, affected your way of life, especially negatively, well, naturally, you wouldn't be too keen on my candidacy, and you could say that for a policy that might affect many a person's background, or condition in life. But, strictly speaking, it's the Constitution. I am not your moral compass, but because we must be realistic about these things, we must address it. Otherwise, why would I even speak to a group of gay people? I would just setup a podium on the street and whomever came to listen, came."

So, let's start with a few broad comments. "There is a substantial group of people who identify as gay, lesbian, or another sexual orientation. I don't get caught up in all the names, because these are personal situations that, frankly, aren't my business. Are they my concern? Well, if there is anything keeping you from living a life in freedom as expressed in the Constitution, then yes, as President, it's my concern.

Let's skip all the history of homosexuality. There is a portion of humans throughout history that have always been gay, in every imaginable group, without regard to gender, race, religion. People are born with a sexual orientation. In some circles, that is not believed but I never chose my sexual orientation, who I am, what is right for me, so can't imagine you did for yourselves. I don't have all the answers in these matters, but we know the truth, and people of character and decency should support the rights of adults to marry whom they wish. Yes, there are some extenuating circumstances, of close relatives and perhaps other matters. But not with most consenting adults. So, okay today, finally, gay people can marry, and deserve the same rights are heterosexual people. When I was a kid, gay people had to hide their identity. Same-sex marriage was a dream, not even a fight.

The group wasn't convinced, as no groups were that spoke with Milt, and the first half used him as a punching bag to vent about the discrimination they felt came from the right. Milt sat there

and listened. At first, there were no questions. They just wanted to smack him around like most all the other groups. When they finished, Milt spoke up. "I'm going to tell you what I tell other minorities. I'm not in your shoes. I'll never know what it's like to be you, but I can tell you this. You deserve the same rights as anybody else. Live the way you want. Besides being gay, I assume you have other cares, about business, employment, healthcare, maybe education. My goal is to make this country as strong as it can be. That's why I believe in fiscal policies that tend to be more conservative, and social policies.
that tend to be more liberal, but with both, there are exceptions. If I'm President, gay people will continue to marry each other, raise children, and live their lives any way they desire, under the law. I believe in equal rights for all adult, U.S. citizens.

The questions moved to the economy and taxes, foreign relations, and as a general rule, the group tended to be more liberal and in favor of more social programs. "How many of you own your own businesses." A few hands went up. My experience with gay friends and acquaintances is that many have advanced degrees and I've known a lot of business owners, doctors, lawyers, artists, and they keep their eye on taxes, and at the end of the day, we may be gay, we may be straight, but we all want to walk on the streets and be safe, and keep as much as our money as we can. We have more in common than we think, and think of it this way, in terms of ever considering voting for me. I piss off just about as many right wingers as left wingers. I believe in equality for all but tend to be a little more fiscally conservative. If you keep a little more of your money with me, that's not a bad thing, and I'm going to do nothing to try and take away any kind of social freedoms you have. That's so last century. The last comment got a smirk from a few. The only applause was done out of courtesy, and that's about it. They didn't hate Milt, but they still saw him as being from the enemy camp, and they couldn't simply trust a guy so quickly.

Dr. Horace Franklin presided over the Congregation at the Mount Zion Baptist Church in Little Rock, one of the largest Black churches in the Southeast. Dr. Franklin had gotten to know Milt through various causes and writings and contacted him about speaking at his service. They had a very pleasant phone call.

"Well, hello, Major Greenbaum", came the voice over the phone. "Oh, please", Milt responded, "Call me Milt", Dr. Franklin. "Only if you call me Horace", Dr. Franklin said and laughed. "Oh, no", Milt answered, but he understood the response. "I have too much respect for you, sir." "And I shouldn't have respect for you?" Dr. Franklin chuckled. "Ha, ha, well I see your point." "We want to be congenial, but we want to show respect. I'll call you Horace but only in private." "Well, that works for me!" Neither man was that vain, and while neither stood on ceremony, they did appreciate the respect allowed to them. Dr. Franklin overcame much to attain his seminary degree, while goodness knows, Milt studied hard and put up with much to become both a lawyer and had sacrificed much to rise in the Army ranks.

"I've been reading all about you", Dr. Franklin said. "How you've been eager to speak to groups of all backgrounds. Share your feelings, speak on difficult topics. How you are going to speak the truth, be critical, not hold back, that the nation needs to hear the harsh truth at times to move forward." "Yes", Milton responded. "A radical idea, isn't it?" "By God, yes", said Dr. Franklin. "It's a most radical idea, and I hope you've invested in body armor." "Well,", Milt said, "I have a bodyguard much of the time." "Yes, but can he protect your mind, your character?" Dr. Franklin said, coyly. "Well, I'm afraid that part will be left to me.

I have dreamt of being in this situation for much of my life. I want to break the mold of the politician. I want to bring people together, really bring them together, by shattering stereotypes, telling the truth, getting people to look at themselves in the mirror and taking responsibility." "Well,", said Dr. Franklin, "that's why I'm calling you. I'd like you to speak to my congregation. Don't hold back, for if you do, don't bother coming. I've heard you speak, so I know where you stand, on African Americans, on our strengths, our weaknesses, and on society, and I want my congregation to hear it. To persuade them, in part. To let them understand some of what I've been telling them, and to hear a different perspective, and I'm telling you now, this is one of those times that you might want to bring one of those bodyguards. We have our share of stubborn people, but it's only by hearing a fresh new perspective on things that people can grow." Milt was impressed to hear the Minister's comments, his passion. They spent a few minutes deciding on a good date, on how he conducts his services, on how he introduces Milt. He wouldn't "leave him hanging out to dry". The congregants would know he was coming, see him there in the front row. Not wonder why a white man was there, but Milt would have to be ready for a protest, of sorts. For disagreement. He had to be prepared to hear dissenting views. Angry views, stories of racism that despite Dr. Franklin's conservative leanings, ideologies and lectures that Milt might need to hear. Things that, as a white man, a wealthy man, a man who has never known hunger, or cold, has never had to hear. Things he will never fully understand despite his reading, or even seeing a portion of it. No, some things must be experienced, discovered first-hand, to understand, and Milt cannot do that. "Milt, I want you here because I believe in your message, and I want my congregants to hear it, but I want you to hear things, too. There are, perhaps, things that YOU must hear, that YOU must work to understand. "Well,", said Milt. "I think that's a good idea."

Milt arrived two weeks later. The congregants were told the week before that Milt would be there, so don't be alarmed when a large white man was sitting in the front row. It wasn't an accident. He said that Governor Greenbaum would be polite, and he expected nothing less from his congregants, but that Milt Greenbaum would challenge them, their beliefs, say some things they might not like, and that they had the opportunity, freedom, and obligation to do the same.

So, Milt showed up in a nice suit and came early. He sat in the front pew while soft organ music filled the hall. He got stares, but people knew he was coming. Milt approached a few near him, said hello, and shook their hands. People were courteous but watched him until the service began. There were some hymns, naturally, and eventually, Dr. Franklin came up and gave a short speech.

"Ok", he began. Today is a special day. A different day, although I suspect that some of the messages will be the same, except I will not be your key speaker this morning. I think you recall that last week, I told you that we would have a guest. Let's go ahead and address the "white elephant in the room". People laughed, and Dr. Franklin said, "Good. We need a little bit of humor. Now, Milton Greenbaum is the Governor of Georgia and a former lawyer and Army Colonel. Milt was a former Major, not a Colonel, but every little bit helped. That's quite a resume, don't you think so? But the Governor, or Colonel, or lawyer isn't happy about everything he sees in the country. He doesn't need to run for President. He can retire if he would like, I would imagine, but he wants to help. I've spoken with him, and I believe he's a good man. You will critique the man, criticize him, judge him for who he is and just as important, who he is not, but like any man, he was born to be who he is. He cannot be you and he cannot be me. He cannot feel your pain, he cannot live as you do, but that doesn't mean that he can't listen to you, and it doesn't mean that he can't be President. After all, we've had a few white Presidents before." A small amount of laughter came from the congregation, but probably less than the Reverand had hoped for. "Let me say one more thing before I bring Governor Greenbaum up to the pulpit. He may tell you some things you don't like or agree with, or believe he's even in a position to say, but we can only grow by experiencing discomfort. We cannot grow when things are easy, only when we are placed outside our comfort zone, and this is precisely why I asked him to come. If he spoke just like me or any of you, or believed just as we all might believe, well then, we wouldn't need him here, would we? So, I ask you to respect this congregation, respect this grand building, respect me, and most importantly, respect yourselves, by extending to Governor Greenbaum the upmost courtesy. That does not mean that you have to accept his opinions on everything, and that you can't respond back. It simply means that you will listen, that you will allow him to speak. Governor, the pulpit is yours."

Governor Greenbaum walked up the pulpit. "Well, Dr. Franklin. Thank you for your hospitality, and to everyone for giving me an opportunity to speak with you briefly today. When I decided to run for President, I wanted to do so in order to be honest, something politicians aren't always known for, and to speak to all kinds of people. So, let's get right to it, and I move quickly.

Number one, as you can see, I am white. That also means that I am not black. I will never know what it is like to be black, so maybe I should turn right around and walk myself out of here, right? No, I don't think so. We're all here, in this country, and some of the things that have happened in this country, in the past, cannot adequately be put into words. The way black people have been treated in this country make a sham out of the Declaration of Independence and of the U.S. Constitution. How do you turn back the clock? That is one of the questions and some of the debate on race relations. I believe, and this is where I meet with a lot of pushback from some people, that you do not turn back the clock. You fix the problem, and you move forward. Easy for me to say, but I'm saying it, and when I speak to the media or to another group, I'll say the same thing. Black people have waited a long time to simply be treated fairly, the same as everyone else. I believe most of our legislation has been changed to reflect that. People ask, "is there systemic racism in the country today, and when I say no, I am attacked. Most of the legislation, or laws, or policies that take the freedoms from black people, which relegate them to second class citizens, are gone. There may be some remaining areas, perhaps even subtle, that if they are there, need to be crushed, removed. But what goes on in the hearts and minds of Americans is something a government cannot change. Only the people can change it. You might sit in the front of a bus and still meet bigotry from others. That is not acceptable, but no government policy will change that, just as it could not change views toward the many other minorities in this country, like Asians, Jews, Catholics, Irish, Italians, Mexicans, and others. No, groups, more importantly, people, must raise themselves up as individuals.

The Reverend walked over to the podium and said. We've put up a microphone in the aisle right there. Would anybody like to ask a question? As if it was rehearsed, all eyes turned to an elderly woman, Josephine Edwards, who was eighty-one years old, and looked it, yet at the same time, she had a steely set of eyes and a straight back. She was not a woman you wanted to play games with. Josephine Edwards was also a famous Little Rock resident. She was one of the "Little Rock Nine", chosen to desegregate Little Rock Central High School as a fifteen-year-old, in 1957.

Josephine Clemmons Edwards was a local hero, to Black residents, and many of the white ones, too.

What a site it was, on September 2, 1957, the night prior to the teens' first day at school. Governor Orval Faubus brought in the National Guard to stop it.  But by September 4th, the students entered, and history was made, despite the tremendous amount of bitterness from the white population.

The way the folks in Little Rock, the Black community, and the church looked at it, Josephine Edwards could do and say anything she wanted to. She earned her stripes, the hard way, and she didn't usually hold back, and not today, as she stepped up to the microphone.

Governor Greenbaum, what in the hell do you know about being Black? How could you, for one minute, ever attempt to walk in our shoes, to know what we've been through, the looks we get every day, the poor treatment, the condescending attitude. You're too young to know about the public humiliation, the separation drinking fountains, sitting in the back of buses, and many things much worse than that. You tell me why we would expect to be led by a man like you?
Milt was mildly taken back, but this was a learning experience for him, even after all these years. All he could do was tell the truth. "Ma'am, you're right. I will never know what it's like to be Black. So, where do we go from here?" He stayed silent. Josephine stiffened. She expected some half-ass "I feel your pain" speech from Milt. "Well,", she continued. "Why should we listen to a word you have to say, then? Why should you lead us?" The Reverand whispered in Milt's ear, "She prefers to be called Mrs. Edwards." Milt began again, "Mrs. Edwards, I began this campaign with only one promise, and that was to tell the truth. So, I will continue to do that. I will never be black. All I can do is treat you, other Black people, and all people, the same way, with courtesy and respect. Those that treat me with any less than respect may get a diminished look back from me, no matter who they are, but since I can never be who you are, what I CAN do is listen, learn, be respectful, and use my experience as a lawyer, Army veteran of twelve years, and Governor, to provide for ALL people, the best leadership I can. Try to make this country a better place to live, and that means for all. A better economy, a healthy job market, a safe nation, and that means safe from foreign enemies and safe from our own citizens that may wish to do you harm. I'm not very good at making high-profile racial speeches or promises. My goal is to treat everyone the same. No special privileges but also, no discrimination, no matter who you are. Absolute freedom and

fairness for all. We can't change the past, only the present and the future. What I will not do, like many politicians before me, is to give you false promises, false hope. I will not offer you unreasonable promises right at election time and then forget you exist all the other days. I will not look down upon you by assuming that without special programs, you do not have the ability to compete. That is racism. I won't sell Black Americans short. I've seen too many extraordinary black men and women in my lives to realize that they just need opportunity on an even playing field, and when you do, great things can happen. But if that playing field is not level, then we need to discuss, and maybe, take action. I will listen. We all must look at ourselves in the mirror and take responsibility for our lives, for our actions, and in this country, freedom offers opportunity, but no guarantees. Do you have another question?"

Josephine stood there for a minute. She finally said, "Famous last words, Governor." "But Mrs. Edwards, I promise nothing different to Black people, or to gay people, or to other groups, except the identical treatment that all Americans should get. Respect, civility, and the same opportunities. What some say is "Freedom of Opportunity, not freedom of outcome." I cannot guarantee the results. This is America and with freedom and opportunity also comes uncertainty. Anything else and there is an imbalance. Turning the tables will only create bitterness with others." Josephine Edwards gave a small smirk and sat down.

Another congregant asked what the Governor would do to pay reparations to Black people. Milt said, "I'll be frank, and I apologize if it comes out the wrong way, but we cannot and should not pay reparations. There's no equitable way to do that. Nobody alive today was a slave, and while I truly understand that the horrors, the brutality of slavery lingers in some ways to this day, we cannot bankrupt the country, or, again, make this an equitable process. I would rather spend time and resources to make sure all schools have the same quality teachers, materials, and are safe, that there are measures in place for

Black people to feel safer in and out of their neighborhoods, and that they have equal employment opportunities. Ladies and gentlemen, as harsh as this sounds, and despite my never fully understanding your history and your predicament, slavery ended a very long time ago, and so has Jim Crow. You must look in the mirror and remind yourself that your success, and that of your children, first lies with you as an individual and as parents. To get the best education you can, to follow our laws, and to raise a family with two parents. No matter what anybody tells you, and no matter how angry you might be with me right now, I do care about your well-being, and only by telling the truth can I help best.

Surprisingly, a woman said, "Amen", and there was a slight giggle from the congregants. Others, however, sat stone faced. To some, it was a slap in the face, and there was nothing Milt would be able to do about it. If he was expecting a slam dunk, he was delusional.

"So, you don't believe that Jesus Christ is our Lord and Savior", came a new question from a second congregant. "No, I don't". A murmur moved through the crowd. "But", Milt answered, "I figured that as a Jew, you knew that but let me explain. First, the most important thing is that I am not running to be your Minister, your spiritual leader. Dr. Franklin does a fine job at that, I imagine," while giving the Reverand a reassuring smile. "I am running to be a government administrator and protect the Constitution. I am not going to affect your freedom to believe in your faith. Besides, have you ever had a service that doesn't include, in addition to Jesus, who was Jewish, Abraham, Issac, and Jacob. Moses?" "No, we don't," said an anonymous voice, which prompted a slight laugh that perhaps broke the tension, somewhat." "You see." said Milt. We have our differences in scripture, but we also have the things we share. The Ten Commandments. God brought that to Moses, for all mankind. That's what matters." "Then what DO you believe? How can you not accept Jesus," came the same questioner. Milton responded again, and naturally, he had had lots of time to think of these things. Telling the truth.

"Ma'am, you are entitled to your belief, and I respect it. I believe in God, but I am not sure of all the details. I was not raised in the concept of a savior as you have been, so I don't subscribe to the story of Jesus as someone other than human. I could be wrong, very clearly, but I decided long ago not to worry about those things. Did Moses part the Red Sea? I don't believe it happened exactly that way, and that's a Jewish story as much as anything else. I do believe in what I think is largely the purpose of these stories. Of treating other humans with respect, not to hurt others, to live the kind of life that God expects us to, to believe in something bigger than ourselves. To walk the Earth with humility. Aren't you sick and tired of politicians who belittle the other candidates, mock them, intimidate them? Many heads shook in the affirmative. "Many voters consider that strength. I consider it a weakness. It takes more strength to affirm your beliefs clearly and if there is an attack on your opponent, you attack their beliefs on the issues, not on a personal level. What has happened to that? Many politicians have told you they share your belief in every regard, but they did not necessarily protect the Constitution or wish to protect your rights as a citizen. That's what I plan to do, so no, I do not share your religious convictions entirely, but I will protect your right to worship as you choose, and I will respect your beliefs. If you have a belief, and it's a peaceful one that does not infringe on others, then it's, frankly, none of my business. I promise not to run for Minister of your church. Don't worry, Dr. Franklin, I've got your back."

Milt eventually sat down, and after a couple more hymns, the service was over. The Reverand took Milt aside and told him who Josephine Edwards was, a member of the Little Rock Nine. Milt was astounded. He knew the story, of course, and didn't think of the fact that he was in Little Rock. He had a profound respect for Josephine Edwards, and wanted to say something, but never had the chance again. "Milt", the Reverand said, "You stood up to her. Most cannot. She's a proud woman, and I would consider a draw with her, a victory for you." The truth was, Milt secretly thought that he won the debate, but then again, who was keeping score?

Some of the congregants shook Milt's hand, and others ignored him, while others, still, gave him a look of contempt. "Well,", Milt thought to himself. "Why should this church be like any other gathering of people. People either see my message, or they think I'm wrong, or maybe they're just too weary, tired of so many disappointments and words of false hope from politicians and others, that they're slow to believe in anything, anymore. Milt felt bad. He remembered as a child, daydreaming about going back in time, to a plantation while a slave was being whipped, grabbing the whip from the white man, and beating him with it, asking him, "Well, you bastard", how does that feel?" He daydreamed about the great Black entertainers, with more talent in their pinky than the fat, overindulgent white audiences there to be entertained, being free to sing and dance on stage, to entertain, and then not even allowed to walk through the front door of an establishment, like a normal human being. Milt wasn't there, but it was certainly the case in places like Clarksdale, Memphis, and Atlanta, not many years before he was born. And then there was a irony of entertainer Al Jolson, perhaps the first "superstar", before Sinatra, Elvis, the Beatles, and Michael Jackson. The famous singer donned black face often in his career, with many today looking back at him with scorn, and yet, he stood up for black entertainers more than any of his contemporaries. So, who could explain those times? His parents and grandparents lived through it, and hated it, but these things had to play out and rely on the efforts of brave people to sacrifice, sometimes by dying, to move the needle of justice, and Milt's family toed the line. Milt suspected they believed that raising a family and helping in their own way, by hiring Black workers and giving back to communities, was the best decision. How many grocery stores would have been built if they, as "trouble-making Jews" pushed the boundaries? They had a good life, and the occasional "pushy Jews" and "greedy Jews", when they had to raise grocery prices like all grocers, when their own costs rose, notwithstanding, the Greenbaum's had lived the American dream. One on one, when they were speaking to customers, and in small groups, the people in their grocery area, their customers, knew the Greenbaum's did their best. They established a strict training program, where every cashier not only said "thank you", but looked the customer in the eye and said, "Thank you. We really appreciate your business and hope you come again, soon".  The chicken sandwich folks from Atlanta had the right idea, but Isidore Greenbaum invented the "courteous cashier" fifty years earlier. Every store had a sign at the exit and said this. To show sincere gratitude. Milt couldn't recall how many times his mother herself would go shopping, perhaps at a clothing store or hardware store, and the cashier didn't establish eye-contact, and didn't say thank you. She wanted to reprimand them, like she would do when a Greenbaum's employee would forget to say thank you in their special way, but she didn't. However, from time to time, once in the car, his mom would talk. "Well, I'll tell you, she said in her Mississippi accent. That girl would NOT be working in a Greenbaum's, not with that poor attitude." Or maybe she would say, "These youngsters don't understand that without their customers, they wouldn't have a job." But usually, she said nothing, but Milt always saw it in her face. Her dad was the more cheerful one, the one willing to laugh off the guy cutting him off on the street, or even to make a comment. Even the one time, a customer said to Milt's dad, on one of his many store visits, "Oh, c'mon Mr. Greenbaum, can't I 'Jew you down' on these steaks?" Milt's Mom would be furious, ready to rumble, so to speak, but his dad would say, "Now, honey, it's a figure of speech, part of the vernacular, and most people don't even realize that it's not exactly a nice thing to say. Just go with the flow. They're customers, remember." Depending on her mood, his mom might remain silent, and other days, the anger would come out, "I don't care. They KNOW we're Jewish. The entire darned state and world knows we're Jewish, and they don't care. We don't need customers like that." His dad might just smile, letting her vent, but other times, he'd voice his opinion slightly firmer, "Honey, you're expecting too much from people, and pumping up your Jewishness too much. We are not innocent of making the occasional prejudicial remark now and then. It's human nature. Doesn't make it right, but if they hated us, they wouldn't shop here." Finally, if Mrs. Greenbaum was still seething, as little Milton once witnessed, she might say, "I don't care. They have to eat. We have the freshest product at the best prices, and they all know it. So, they have contempt for us, yet they come here because WE treat them well." "Well honey", Milt's dad might finish off with. "We live pretty well because of our customers. Cut them some slack, and honey, I love it when your feathers are ruffled a little bit," and he'd kiss her on the cheek. She'd give him the smallest of smiles, and say, "I'm completely serious. We deserve respect. "Everybody does", said Milt's dad. "No, they don't" his wife would insist, and Milt's dad would laugh. On occasion, everybody would. You worked hard, every day, and did your best, and even when you did that, there would be people who didn't care about your happiness, or your desire for respect. Many wanted you to fail. They were unhappy themselves. Milt's dad told him what his own father told him, "You can't control the feelings of other people. All you can do is do your best, play by the rules, and treat others with respect, even when they don't treat you the same." Milt, at times, thought that was unreasonable, as a kid. Why turn the other cheek? But eventually, he realized that he wasn't turning the other cheek. He was preserving his own self-respect, but that took many years of maturation and reflection. It was never easy, but sometimes, doing the right thing wasn't an easy task.

More speeches around the country place. An interesting one happened at a large Black church, with a conservative Pastor that warned him ahead of time what things might be like. Milt started by saying, "I don't know if I'm facing friends or opponents. I've never been in your shoes, so I can't pretend to say that I understand what you face, or how you feel. I believe everyone should be treated the same, no matter how bad the past has been. I also believe that it does no good to punish people today for the sins of people now dead. The dead ones may deserve it, but they're dead. Is that easy for me to say? Yes, very easy, but is it true? Yes, I think it's true. I believe that Black people are every bit as good and often better than white people in every discipline you can mention, be it medicine, science, the arts, the law, sports, and business. Why? Because I've seen it. We all have. It's out there. Here's the negative part of what I have to say. I believe some people feel lost, angry, and they fail themselves and others. They fail their family and society. There is a very sad truth that no matter what has happened to you, no matter how terrible and unfair life has been to you or your people, whomever they may be or whatever that means. The truth is, if you want to rise in society and become equal, you must not only perform as equally as the others you're compared with. You have to outperform them, just to catch up. Think of it this way. If a car is ahead of you on the road, and you want to catch them, maybe pass them, you'll never do it if you both maintain the same speed. You will have to go faster just to catch up. Only then can you pass them. The laws and society may have come about as far as they are going to come, and now, it's mostly up to you. It can be done, and it is being done every day. Imagine telling someone in 1960 that just after the start of the 21st century, a Black man would be President.

If you vote for me for President, I will do all I can to make sure no laws or practices in society hold you back. I will not back special privileges or rights for any group. I won't lie to you. Oh, for veterans, but they earned that right by serving in the military. There may be programs to help people catch up. I will always listen, and I will try to compromise, but if we are to ever get to a day where we're color-blind, or as close we can be to it, then we have to begin acting that way. You are all my fellow citizens. I can see that you are Black, but until I have a very good reason to act otherwise, you will have the same kindness and respect from me as I would give to anyone else. This nation needs Black people to thrive, to excel. I want that, and I believe it will continue to happen, but attitudes among some must change. White attitudes and yes, black attitudes. Get your children to believe in themselves. Keep your families together. If you think that I'm just a clueless white man, then I'm sorry, but I'm being honest with you. I want nothing more than for Black people to look upon America as a place of great opportunity and happiness, with scores of successful business owners and leaders in all areas of society. I don't want to hand you a bill of goods. I won't lie to you. You have to earn it and prejudice will never go away. You have to work ahead and be successful in spite of it. Thank you for your time today."

Milt got a larger round of applause than he thought he would, because the audience, like him or not, believed he was being sincere. Some thought he just didn't get it, but they believed that he believed the words he was saying. Two or three came up to him later and said, in so many words, "You know, Governor, you're right about many of the things you said. I've always believed it. But it's a long road. The trust isn't there, the enthusiasm, the hopefulness, it's not there for everyone." Milt would answer, "Yes, sir. That's what I hear a lot. We have to keep trying, somehow."

Milt actually sought out an audience at a mosque, but the back-and-forth negotiations never materialized, and Dan practically begged him not to do it. It was looking for trouble in more ways than one, but if Milt wanted to address the problems in the Middle East, he had his chance during one of four town halls he conducted in different parts of the country. A question came up from the many audience members about how he would settle what seemed to be the permanent problem in the Middle East. It was a gentler question than the inflammatory shouts from pro-Palestinian Americans, about the conduct of Israel and how Milt, a Jew as well as an American politician, would do nothing to show fairness in the cause.

"The land we know as Israel today is the ancient land of the Jews. According to Exodus, in the Bible, God freed the Hebrews from bondage in Israel, and led them to the holy land. Outside the Bible, artifacts and landmarks show the Jews in this land since that time. Arabs came to occupy the land for hundreds of years. Longer, perhaps. After the horrors of the Holocaust, the British and the Allies carved out a section of land for the Jews. Arabs were displaced. Some Jews were not in favor of a nation. They have, and some still do, believe that Judaism is a religion and should never represent a nation. But the nation of Israel was established regardless, in 1948, on a piece of land that is a sliver when compared to all the Arab land. It was far from perfect, but the Jews were returned, and have turned a desert into a miracle. Great universities and thriving cities. But the Arabs have never accepted the change, which many predicted, and there has never been peace. Both sides have a claim, so the answer is a two-state solution, not continuous violence. The Jews want it. The Palestinians do not. The term "From the River to the Sea", is interpreted by many to mean that Palestinians will only be satisfied when the Jews are driven out, perhaps dead or alive. That is not an option, certainly not for the Israeli's, not for most Americans, and not for me. Does Israel overstep, in defending their land? Even Israeli's argue about which policies are best. Arguments among the Likud, Yesh Atid, and others. Israel may be in the wrong, at times, but they have also shown great restraint. Who are we to speak for them when every day, they are faced with potential violence and rockets flying above? They are not the ones celebrating when our twin towers fell on 9-11. Yet, we have given money to both Israel and Arab lands. Whether I was Jewish or not, Israel has remained an ally, a friend. Other Presidents have said it. I will say it. Israel deserves to exist as a nation, and the Arab nations must recognize that if there is to be lasting peace. But all people in the region should have the chance to live free and live in peace. My focus will be on our own nation, but we will be a partner in peace, if that's what the nations in the Middle East are willing to do. If they attack, then Israel has the right to defend itself. I would say to the Palestinians, you deserve a seat at the table, if you pledge peace. You deserve to be heard, always, but you must condemn terrorism, and you must formally recognize Israel. At that time, Israel must also step up to the plate, and real compromise can begin to take place, and remember, with compromise comes some pain, some sacrifice, and commitment. As long as Palestinian leaders vow death and fail to recognize Israel, there cannot be a lasting peace. Regardless of my faith, two sides cannot find peace if one refuses to even recognize that the other exists. How can it? Israel exists. It's a nation, and yet, even its citizens condemn their own government for some of their policies, just like we do here. Peace can be achieved if both sides want it. Both sides. I would not suggest you look to me, if I become President, to force these people to get along. That is up to them, and I will not take the side of anti-Zionists. I am a Zionist myself. I support Israel as a nation, but I would also support the right of the Palestinian people to have their own nation, and live free and in peace. If they show they are committed, then as American President, I will offer the services of the United States in assisting with an agreement any way that I can. "

"Jesus", said Dan. "Why did you have to tell them that you were a Zionist?" Dan complained later. "Why not?" said Dan. Is that like saying I'm a Devil worshipper?" "Bingo, you nailed it," Dan replied. "I support the existence of Israel, just like I support the existence of Great Britain, Argentina, and South Africa." "It's not the same thing," Dan added, "Well", said Milt, it should be. What's done is done. You know, just because I'm Jewish doesn't mean I'm going to slam Israel every chance I get, to prove that I don't take sides. I DO take sides on this one, but it's mostly because Israel has been a friend to America, during the Cold War and other times. Forget about the religion part." "I don't think some people can forget about the religion part," Dan said. "Well, some things I can't help, and the Presidents of the past have said the same thing as me." "Yes, perhaps," said Dan, but

74

their names were Clinton, Nixon, Kennedy, Carter…. not GREENBAUM." "Oy", was all Milt could say, a word he generally detested.

# The National Debate

Eventually, a series of two debates between Greenbaum and Madison were set up. After several primaries, the two were within 10% of each other in gathering the necessary delegates to win the nomination. Even though there was a swell of support for Milt, as people tired of the division, and many self-proclaimed Libertarians pulled for Milt, the conservative media and more assertive groups held firm for Madison over the "Rino" Greenbaum. These Republicans didn't want harmony or even respect among those in Washington. They wanted a slam dunk, like many on the other side. "A vote for Milt Greenbaum is a vote for liberal policies and a weaker America".

Both sides got plenty of coaching. Madison was warned to keep it civil. Portray Greenbaum as a nice man, a veteran, a hard worker, but naïve in the way of the Federal government, of how treacherous the other side was. There was no doubt about it, why would a Democratic voter abandon the ideals they love, which were more "progressive" than ever before, for a watered-down version of liberal policies? It will be a slam dunk for the Democrats.

At one point, Madison forgot how politicians once treated each other, and called Greenbaum a "coward" for failing to adequately address some of the nation's most severe issues. Milt let him speak, then answered him. "Typically, I would address Mr. Madison, or anyone else, directly, but since there are rules to the debate, rules not usually followed today, I will respond to the moderator. About me being a coward. I take issue with that because it isn't true. It is easy to insult a fellow politician, as Mr. Madison has done. I'm used to it. I also served twelve years in the Army. Mr. Madison has not. I've also had my battles in a courtroom. Trust me, I have thick skin. I can take the insults, and I expect them in politics. I like to think that when you insult, it's because you don't have a good solution or answer. But I made a promise to the nation that I would act differently. I would attack policies, not people. I'm not afraid to insult Mr. Madison right back, but I'm not a coward simply for looking for solutions that will help as many people as possible, or a coward because there might be a compromise. To me, that's smart, that's leadership, not cowardice." Point for Greenbaum.

Greenbaum would venture off the beaten path. He would remain cordial. While he wouldn't blame Madison for extreme views, he would paint him as having the same policies that continue to divide the country.

The debates, for better or worse, were "yawn-fests". Just as predicted, Madison praised Greenbaum, from a hard-working, industrious family, and Army veteran who served his nation for twelve years. A Major and a Lawyer, but (with all due respect) incorrect in his assessment that bending over backward to the other side, and making compromises on bad ideas, would simply make the outcome bad.

"I commend Governor Milt Greenbaum, Major Greenbaum. He's a good man, and I am not here to attack his character, which is unblemished and one we can all be proud of, but even the Governor can agree that the stakes are high. This is the Presidency and too much is at stake not to take a strong stand on positions of importance. The Governor, and again, I must issue harsh attacks on his platform, and not him personally, believes in giving up too much in the way of very poor ideas by the Democrats that will hurt this nation for years to come. And I believe that he will be soundly defeated by progressive Democrats who do not exactly specialize in the common sense that Governor Greenbaum used as a title for his book. They are far to the other side, and it will take a different approach to keep them out of the White House. A tough resolve and a tough platform. Milt Greenbaum's platform, not the man, but his platform, is weak.

And that is how Steve Madison eventually won the nomination. Naturally, the Democratic Candidate used all of this to point out that the Republicans didn't know a good thing when they saw it, in Milt Greenbaum, but agreed that Greenbaum was too indecisive (but in the other direction).

But boy, Milt's supporters loved the guy. Too many rallies to count, and Milt generally showed up. People loved the idea of compromise, getting along, freedom, and an end to preference of any kind due to minority status of some kind. His supporters said that Milt was everything that was right about America, and the other candidates represented the extreme views that were polarizing and dividing the country.

Maybe it was because Americans in 2024 have come to believe that America is no longer the land of hard work and opportunity. Maybe they believed that only a large central government can solve our problems, and maybe they believed that eking out a living, but surviving was better than taking risks and thriving. Competition was seen as "mean" by too many, and further efforts and programs to "humanize" the nation took place. The nation was used to seeing idealistic young college people from the Vietnam era, before and after that, but typically, people settled down, got jobs, realized that they had to compete to win, had to compromise to get along with others, and they most certainly realized that life wasn't fair and that there was no such thing as a free lunch. But somewhere along the way, the politicians convinced them in this country, like they did in Russia, China, and Venezuela, that the government was the answer to their prayers, and when only the government officials got rich, they were left with empty shelves, smashed dreams, and in some cases, dead civilians who dared to disagree. In the United States, they weren't there yet. They were only at the "cancel" stage. Banning and changing of words, preaching peace and love while blocking highways and demanding an end to free speech on college campuses and elsewhere.

The President overseas the Executive Branch of the Federal government and is tasked with protecting the rights in the United States Constitution. That is any President's task.

"I've thought long and hard about emotional questions, difficult questions, or volatile questions that the public want to hear answers to." Milt asked the CNN reporter. "Have you ever heard of the word, 'otiose'?" "No" said the reporter. "Well,", said Milt, it's an old English word, and it means, basically, "producing no useful result." That is how I look at questions like a person being gay. I firmly believe a gay person is born gay, but really, why are we discussing this? It serves no useful purpose. Gay people have existed for all time. Now we could argue, or discuss, sexuality, reproduction. Shouldn't every man desire a woman, sexuality, because the entire purpose of sex is to procreate, and it feels so we do it? If it was painful, people wouldn't do it and humans would die out. So, if it's for procreation, then why do some people have sex with the same gender. I don't know, but it has always been, and it has nothing to do with how I would run the country. So, it serves no purpose. Now, it may be a very important social subject, and for me to say 'I don't care' about doesn't mean to don't like gay people, or care about the discrimination against them. No. It means that it is not a determining factor for anybody becoming President. We need a new phrase to mean 'not serving any useful purpose. Just because I am a Republican, and to some, I am meant to be hurtful and not understanding of people's feeling, which doesn't mean that it's true. We must not be afraid to bring up difficult topics in this arena, the political arena, but I don't have to walk past a person who I know is transgender, a biological man trying to appear and live happily as a woman and mock them. It's wrong on every level, it's deliberately unkind, meant to harm them. Does that mean I agree with allowing them to compete in athletics against women? No, I disagree with it very strongly, in fact. But it makes no sense to embarrass and humiliate people. We're better than that. But that doesn't mean I'm going to agree with some the nonsense I see in policymaking, and I'll attack those ideas.


In the end, the candidacy of Milton Greenbaum can be summed up in his own words from his book, "Common Sense".

"I knew when I set out that people had shifted into two camps. Oh sure, I saw society as sort of a bell curve, oh, you remember the bell curve from school. Most people clumped together in the middle. The vast majority think the same. Then, a small number all the way to one side, and a small number all the way to the other side, forming a graph that appears like a big bell. Most people want to be happy. They want comfort, they like good food, to be entertained, to feel good physically, mentally. You know, all those basic things. Naturally, how they achieve these things, these goals, may vary greatly. Some man might love football and cold beer, and never to dress in anything fancier than a clean t-shirt and a pair of comfortable jeans. Some man might like Mozart and fine wine, a well-tailored suit, and Shakespear. Different ways to achieve the same thing. Happiness. Most Americans didn't really care what others did to achieve their happiness as long as they were left alone to achieve theirs. But politicians, oh yes, the politicians. They wanted power, and the best way to do that was to divide and conquer. If the two parties were similar, well, then, how could the politician win and stay in power? Why would a Republican come out and say that while he found abortion a terrible thing, whether or not to have one, under most circumstance, was in the hands of the woman. She had the final say. That seemed like common sense, even if the person who objected was disgusted by it. The same with sexual preferences. A straight man didn't need to go around telling people that he would find sex with another man a terrible thing. That falls under the category of, well, maybe there's not a word for it. Milt had a very good gay friend and they joked about it. His friend said, 'Oh, it feels great, you should try it, and Milt said, "It's just disgusting to me." "Well,", said his friend, "I think sex with a woman is disgusting!" "Are you crazy?" asked Milt. "Sex with a woman, the right woman, of course, is one of the greatest things in the world." "No way, no way." And Milt and his friend would laugh about it. It was interesting to Milt. He could never understand it, but his friend wasn't upset with him, and Milt respected him. There was simply something different about the ways they were designed. Two men. Two completely different sets of circumstances. And yet, they could both enjoy a good steak. A stupid comparison. Who cares what you think? You see, this was how Milt was constructed. Nothing is wrong with the truth and yet, there were times telling the truth simply wasn't necessary. Milt understood that a transgendered woman was really a man. Even the most ardent supporters, the ones that graduated from Harvard and yet said that a woman could have a penis. Well, they ALL know better. Yes, all of them. But they go along because they believe in humanity. Of dignity for these people born with an overwhelming feeling that, well, their bodies didn't match their minds. Their souls. Something wasn't right, but acting out the way they wish was real and true for them gave them happiness. Well, then so what if we go along for their happiness? Would you be arrested for trying to let someone find happiness? What kind of jail sentence would that be? Yes, there were times when Milt wanted to say, "Cut the crap, you're really a man. Because it was true. This person really was a man, and everybody knew that no matter what they said out loud. And there were times when Milt felt it was bad for society. I mean, at one what point does this hurt families, or children? Then there was the question of what was being called "Gender Affirming Care". Drugs or surgery for minors. What if they changed their minds? Well, Milt felt more strongly about this, that you had to wait until a child became an adult, but what if the child was experiencing severe angst, and you were the parent? It was easy to speak to others, Milt thought.

Sometimes, people are faced with extraordinary circumstances. A parent, more than anything else in the entire world, wants their children to be happy, or another way to say it, the want to remove all the pain of their children, and to hell what others think. Republican, Democrat, Libertarian, or whatever political ideology you want to claim, Milt had a way of looking hard at both sides. "What if this were me?" He was good at that. But looking at both sides was only important for a candidate if they could pick a side.

But Milt wanted to try something different before he died. He didn't think he could win because in today's politics, and hell, maybe it has always been this way, you cannot venture out into that "no man's land". When you are firmly within your own trench, in your own political bunker, you are surrounded by comrades, from thick walls or solid Earth that protects you from the weapons of the opposition. The political mortar shells. Your comrades are by your side. You constituents who agree with you love you. So, you band together and try to win that small stretch of land in the middle. The "no man's land", because your side isn't going anywhere, and the other side, well, it's not going anywhere either, so the war is won by winning that small land in the middle. Of course, over time, the plateau can shift. It seems like it happened overnight, but probably not.

So, the Presidential "experiment" of Milt Greenbaum failed, as he thought it probably would. Steve Madison, a former Republican Governor himself, had no trouble accepting the strategy set forth for him by his handlers. "Milt Greenbaum is weak. He has taken a dangerous middle ground in the hope of getting reasonable people to consider all sides of the many challenges America faces. He has challenged the people to stop, consider the other person's side. He has taken a conservative view in most cases, but he has been willing to always consider compromise, to always listen, to have the courage to say, "I don't know", and above all, to show respect when dealing with opponents, the public and everyone he meets. In other words,

Milt Greenbaum has opened himself up to complete destruction by any common Republican who will stick to the party's speaking points. To the Democrat, he doesn't go nearly far enough, and to the Republican, he is a "Rino", practically a traitor.

Madison, at every turn, portrayed Greenbaum as weak and indecisive. Under a Greenbaum Presidency, foreign leaders who show us no respect, political opponents would mock him and trounce him, other nations would constantly test our resolve, and even Wall Street, who hated anything speculative, anything that rocked the boat, would consider him too risky. There was nothing but disaster ahead in a Greenbaum Presidency. Frankly, as bad, even as a Democratic Presidency. The Democrats had an easy time as well, portraying Greenbaum as a wolf in sheep's clothing, a hardline Republican from the red state of Georgia, from a super wealthy family who never knew what it was like to struggle. A man thinking he could try to fool American. He was weak, indecisive, and his ideas of compromise would leave Americans nowhere.

The moderator brought up abortion. There was no question it would be on the agenda, in spite of much of the public being sick hearing about it. Minds were rarely changed, and each side was able to state their case, at least in their own minds, making the subject of abortion an open and shut case. For many women, it was the most fundamental case of individual rights. No government had the right to tell a woman what she could do with her own body. It mattered not that this wasn't about altering the body, getting a tattoo, having an operation of some kind, breast augmentation. And it mattered not that it was a fetus, the development of a new human, growing inside the body of that human. After six weeks, a heartbeat. Soon after, fingers, toes, a head, a body. No, it was determined by this group that it wasn't a human being. Not yet anyway. Ignore what could be seen in a sonogram. Ignore, the tiny hands and fingers, the by-product, the waste what was left, removed, after the abortion.

Milt struggled with abortion. He hated it. All the talk about the sanctity of life from the Jews. The prayers, the hymns, the many instances of enemies in the Bible vowing to destroy the Jews, and the Jews prevailing with the help of God. The holocaust. Even in the arts. In "Fiddler on the Roof," life was celebrated for all in the song "To life, to life, L'Chaim." The thought of a fetus, a baby, denied that life, the chance to laugh, to run in the sun, to have that first, amazing feeling when you fall in love, to make love, to raise children, even to fail and fight and redeem yourself. All these parts of life, good and bad, were at the disposal of the people now deciding that that the unborn were not worthy of what they could today experience. A life. A chance, an opportunity. No matter what the inconvenience of parenthood was, it wasn't more important than the life of another human being. Milt couldn't help but feel this way. All the talk and all the understanding he could muster could not change what he ultimately felt. Not a religious man, Milt still looked for an answer in the Jewish texts. He found conflicting statements that frustrated him terribly.

In the Talmud, a collection of Jewish legal materials, it states: "Until 40 days from conception, the fetus is merely water." Science tells us that a heartbeat can be detected in 5-6 weeks, making it around the same time.  In Jewish law, a fetus attains the status of a full person only at birth. Milt was able to find conflicting statements on when a soul entered the body, which Milt didn't believe in anyway, but even still, it pointed to the fact that in his mind, men wrote the scriptures and couldn't decide fully on the matter of abortion, because they were men.

In the end, Judaism has never made a definitive statement on abortion, although he had to admit that the religion allowed for it, at least under certain circumstances. The religion put the life of the mother first, and in other instances, approved of abortion for medical and even mental anguish, but at the same time, there was no proof that abortion was favored in any way. But there was more than enough in the interpretation to convince both Rabbi's and Jews in general that abortion was not to ever be banned, and not up to a government agency. After many years of private thought, Milt determined that if he ever went into politics, he would simply tell the truth, that he felt terribly saddened over abortion. If the mother and fetus were not suffering a medical issue, then it was wrong to do, but ultimately, he felt that the woman had to have the ability to make the decision, and he certainly didn't want the government to make it.

It was in this situation that actually provided acceptance by the majority Democrats with respect to the candidacy of Milt Greenbaum. He didn't "like" abortion. Well, who cares? He was pro-choice, and that's all they wanted. Of course, the Republican line was different, at least as portrayed by the media (even though many Republicans felt as Milt did), and he got hammered for not demanding that abortion be banned outright.

Milt spoke his views. He tried to be brief. It wasn't easy. "I have given the public my views on abortion for years now. Being such a controversial subject, my views aren't welcome for all in my party, but I've thought long and hard about it, and I've struggled. I believe in the sanctity of life. If astronauts discovered a single-celled organism on Mars, it would be hailed by the world as "Life discovered on Mars." But a fetus, even with a beating heart, and ten visible fingers and toes, is considered, even in some religious texts, as "not fully human". If it means, "not fully developed", well, we know that's true, but it is certainly a potential life, and I believe that that life deserves the same chance at life that we all have, so who are we to make this life and death decision? Yet, many Americans believe that a woman should have the right to make this important decision. I agree that I don't want the government to decide this, but I see a fetus for what it is in my mind, and that's a life, a state or condition we were all in once, and we were a chance to live, to love, and with abortion, that fetus is killed. It saddens me and I am against it. I am not talking about medical issues or rape, but as a general rule, I am against it, but after so many years of thought, I would not vote to ban abortion. In the end, the mother must make that choice. It is not a "cop out" as so many like to say about me. I would like to spearhead an initiative to place more emphasis on education, prevention, and easing the adoption rules. We used to say, "make abortion safe, legal, and rare." I'd like to get back to that. That's all I can say right now on the subject.

Then, it was Madison's turn, and he took full advantage. "I'll make it simple, everyone. I believe in life, and I believe that abortion is murder. The Bible says not to kill, and I believe that. Governor Greenbaum claims to tell the truth, and that he's reasonable, but with this "pro-choice" agenda of his, he's complicit, or would be, in the murder of all these unborn babies. Let him squirm his way of this, but at least with a President Madison, you'll have a President who's not afraid to tell you how he stands, whether you like it or not."

# Abortion

If Milt thought the abortion issue was over, he was sadly mistaken. Dan received a call from Melissa Bierman, host of a national news show known to lean left, like most in the media. Milt flat-out refused to go on this show, but Dan agreed to step-in. Abortion was still a hot topic, as if often is, due to a near total-ban of the procedure by a southern state already ridiculed by other areas for being "backward". Ms. Bierman wanted Dan to discuss Milt's position on abortion, once again, and she would have what she promised to be a "well-balanced" panel of advocates, both pro-choice to pro-life, to use two of the "nicer" words to describe it. "Melissa", Dan replied, "the Governor's position on abortion has been well-established. He finds abortion a terrible act, but has not, and will not propose a ban, only a ban on late-term abortions. He realizes that abortion is a highly delicate subject, prone to an abundance of circumstances, and as much as Governor Greenbaum advocates for more aggressive education and steps to greatly reduce abortion, he believes it should remain safe and legal in all states, subject to the conditions I have mentioned. He is saddened by abortion and the death of a fetus, which he considers a human being, but is not going to overstep his authority as a public servant. That is his stance, and as important as it is, it has been beaten to death." Melissa answered, "Oh, c'mon, Dan. Milt Greenbaum is down in the polls and isn't likely to get the Republican nomination. He's seen as too wishy-washy, and any chance he can get to gain additional exposure, for free, mind-you, are a plus. At least ask him yourself and get back to me by tomorrow at noon, because we've got deadlines. As you know, we discuss hot topics, and those topics cool down, and Dan, have you seen my ratings? I'm number one in my time slot. Give the Governor a platform to speak. One way or another, his name will come up on the show. He's running for President, after all, and all the positions of the leading contenders will be brought up. Dan responded, "He can't be everywhere, Melissa. I'm his campaign manager, and I'll step in. He has faced tough audiences everywhere. He's not ducking but he has made his belief clear."

"Milt, it's a trap. I'm telling you. Have you seen her show? It's part "Meet the Press" and "Jerry Springer. I'll get my say if I can blast your way through whatever guests are there to come after you and keep them from talking. I'm telling you as sure as the Moon has rocks, that she'll bring on the most pro-abortion advocate she can find, and then the most hard-right pro-lifer she can find, and for the chance to get onto a top-ranked show, she'll have her pick.

But Milt has the last word, and the "man of compromise" had Dan sit in, in his place. The host had no choice. It was the campaign manager or nothing.

"Eye on Politics" with Melissa Bierman, was indeed a top show, and the network ran a number of ads in the three days leading up to the event. Melissa wanted to run the show sooner, but at a staff meeting, the higher-ups wanted a chance to market the show. Even Melissa felt that if it took place less than a week after the controversial abortion opinion of the state in question, it would be okay, although she preferred to hit hard and fast, usually the same or next day. This would already be "stale", but the promise of Milt's campaign manager would whet the appetite of viewers. Milt sat alone, sipping on a Leinenkugel Summer Shandy, which had just become available for the season.

Dan was ushered into the studio by an executive producer, in the sparsely decorated studio, which included an audience of about 200 people. It proved to be a more difficult ticket to get once the news got out, and some extra security was on hand. Audience members would not be allowed to ask questions, and Melissa Bierman made some opening comments to the audience before the panelists came out. After thanking them, she said that the show today would be covering abortion, and it might get "a little heated". She asked that they please refrain from comments, from booing, from jeers, or screaming. If for any other reason, to make sure that the panelists' opinions could be heard for the home audience. Anyone disrupting the show would have to leave. Metal detectors had long been a staple at this, and most all network studios. It wasn't so much violence the studio worried about. It was obnoxious behavior, although that wasn't always bad for ratings. It did wonders for Jerry Springer, but Melissa figured there would be more than enough fireworks on stage.

A little theme music, and the show started, and what an audience. Melissa began. "Well,", she said, "This will be a show, I believe, to remember, but we'll see. The subject is a familiar one, abortion." Melissa put her own spin on it, "Is it a fundamental right of a woman to do what she wishes with her own body, or will forces in both state and federal government continue its attack on the precious reproductive rights on women? Do we live in a free society, or not? Well, apparently, there are forces that believe the government should control a woman's body, as they have controlled other aspects of a woman's life for over 200 years in this country. Tonight, we have a balanced panel, as we strive to do here, whether people believe that or not. First, on my left, no pun intended, but that's where they sit, is actress Wendy Simon, certainly one of the most recognize pro-choice women's advocate in the entertainment industry, and I see Wendy, you've dressed appropriately for the occasion." Wendy Simon, laughing as she did so often, was wearing a dress that had splattered on it, "I love abortion." "That's right, Melissa. I'm for abortion rights and I'm not afraid to shout it and shove it down the throats of the oppressive, right, and shove it down the throats of all men, who have absolutely no say in the matter. As a matter of fact, I've had three abortions, and they were just fabulous." Even in the left-leaning audience, there were some groans. It was no surprise that Melissa and her producer want the radical as well as the more moderate, on both sides, but people had to remember, that this was entertainment, and without controversy and ratings, Melissa wouldn't stay on the air, so people could say what they wanted. Melissa brought in the ratings.

"Hmm, okay", said Melissa. "Well, we'll address your enthusiasm during the show, as well as some other opinions. You can count on that." "Hey," said Simon. "Bring it."

"We also have Joan Baxter, the Director of "Woman Care", a progressive advocacy group aimed at providing medical, legal, and other service to women. "Joan, where's your dress, you know, your message?" Joan smiled. It wasn't the time to laugh. Not this show. "Well, Wendy is entitled to her message the way she wants to provide it. We at Woman Care are about women, supporting them, doing what we can to make sure they lead free, productive lives, fighting for their well-being, whether that's reproductive health, general health, in the courts, in the office place, wherever a woman needs assistance." "Okay," so in the abortion debate, and of course, I think we know your stance, but for the record, why don't you tell our audience. "Certainly," Joan said. We believe in woman's rights, and that includes the difficult decision to have an abortion, regardless of the circumstances. We're wives, and we're mothers, and celebrate motherhood. We are not a "pro" abortion group. That is an incorrect way of describing us and it is only one area for us." "But you do support abortion rights". "Yes, unquestionably", Joan said, "We are pro-choice. That is what we are. We believe that abortion is a private matter, a critically important decision that belongs to a woman." Melissa played devil's advocate, "But, obviously, you're not against motherhood," the sarcasm being clearly to everybody. "NO,"

90

said Baxter, "and we make that clear. We love mothers, and we advocate for extended maternity leave and other benefits for mothers, before and after birth. We are all about choice, plain and simple, and for defending the rights of woman, not to make their choices for them, and we fight against any oppressive group, government or otherwise, that tries to do that." "But", Bierman continued, "isn't the right to an abortion something to celebrate, like Wendy has expressed?". "We celebrate freedom, and we celebrate women's rights. We don't celebrate abortion". "But you celebrate the murder of innocent babies", came a harsh rebuke from the other side of the stage. There was a splattering of boos from the audience. "Okay, now", said Bierman. "One guest at a time, and I caution our audience to refrain from any disturbances. Since a comment was made, let us shift our attention and introduce the two members on my right, again no pun intended, but it is what it is. Charles Nelson, Director of the American Pro-Life League, and Baptist Minister. Reverand Nelson, you clearly have a differing view of abortion, which is why we asked you to sit on the panel. Could you elaborate further. "Ms. Bierman, the Bible makes it very clear in the Ten Commandments, 'Thou shall not kill.' By every imaginable process, scientific or otherwise, life begins at conception and an abortion is 100% murder. It is a barbaric procedure that would sicken the very people that treat it with such frivolity, and it is an abomination against God." The audience, not expecting anything different from the Reverand, surprisingly stated silent. "Well, Reverend", Bierman continued, you don't believe that woman should have the right to make this decision about their own body?" The Reverand continued, "but it is NOT her body. A fetus may reside inside of a woman's womb, and may need the mother for development, without question, but it is also a separate entity, its own body, its own skeletal system, and from the point of conception,  a wonderous DNA blueprint has been formed that with God's help, will result in the birth of a child, the most blessed event our world can creates, and an abortion is outright murder. In my eyes, it is not a choice, as you say, any more than my choice to go out into the audience and kill one of your members," That prompted a nervous laugh. "Okay", Melissa said, "We get it. You're anti-choice." "No", said the Reverand, "Don't play word games with me", I am anti-murder. "But you're okay with the murder by electrocution of inmates on death row." The Reverand was already agitated, which Bierman took great pride in. Milt listened at home and took notes. "You are comparing apples to oranges", the Reverand said. "You cannot compare the life of an innocent baby to that of a cold-blooded killer. That is not murder. That is justice." "Okay", said Melissa, "Call it what you may". Let's move on to perhaps the man of the hour, perhaps, and Presidential candidate, Governor Milton Greenbaum of Georgia. Sitting in for the Governor is his National Campaign Manager, Dan Bennett. Dan, such a shame that the Governor didn't want to stand up for himself here." She did exactly what she promised she wouldn't do. "Melissa, we spoke about this. Dan had another obligation today, and he has faced every critique on this and all subjects, from the very beginning of his campaign, and he has made his views crystal clear. We agreed you wouldn't try this baloney, and here you are, reneging on your promise. Governor Greenbaum has made his position very clear since entering the political arena eight years ago. He is saddened by abortion. He believes, as the Reverand does, that life begins at conception, and he views an abortion as a terrible, sad event. However, ultimately, he believes this very difficult decision belongs with the mother. There are many circumstances in which a woman might come to this decision. He believes an abortion for the sake of birth control, or bad timing, or even for financial reasons, is wrong. That is his opinion, and when he's President, He'll do he can introduce policies to reduce its occurrence, but he does not support the ban of abortions." "But if a woman wants an abortion, she should be allowed to have one, up to birth?" "No, he does not say up to birth," Dan responded. "But", Bierman continued, you just said that it is a woman's choice. "To a point", continued Dan. "He believes there should be some limits, fair limits, which include the procedure occurring the end

of the first trimester." "And then, he'd ban it," Bierman
continued. Dan said, "That is up to the states." "Oh, that's
bullshit", said, finally, Wendy Simon. "Wendy, please be careful
with your language." "Oh, who cares?" Simon added. "First
chance this guy gets as President, he'll ban abortion, and it's
none of his business what a woman does with her body, or
when. When has Milty ever been knocked-up, Mr. campaign
manager?" Dan said nothing. Let this jackass hang herself. He
made his point clear whether the panel liked it or not. Bierman
spoke again, "The President cannot ban abortion, and the
Supreme Court has already made its decision on Roe v. Wade."
"The Supreme Court can go fuck itself", came the response from
Simon. "Wendy", that only gets taken out and it's a good
reminder of why the show isn't live, but please, control
yourself." That in itself was bullshit, because it's exactly the
response Bierman wanted more of. Bierman continued,
"Reverand, you're known to side with Republican and
conservative causes, yet Governor Greenbaum, while stating his
personal disdain for abortion, nevertheless believes it should
remain legal, a decision left to women. Doesn't that conflict
with your views?" "Well," the Reverand started back up. "The
Governor is not my choice for the Presidency. He is a weak-
minded man we like to call a Rino. A man who knows exactly
what abortion is yet doesn't have the fortitude to call it what it
is, and that's the murder of an innocent baby." Dan stiffened,
"Ms. Bierman, do I get to respond?" Bierman smelled blood in
the water, and the fact that it was the two Republicans made it
even better." "Of course,", said Bierman. "Thank you", said Dan.
"Reverand, Milt doesn't like abortion. You're right, it's the death
of a living, human being, and the decision of abortion should
reside with the mother, but regrettably, they cannot make that
decision. I'd like to let all of you know, our moderator, Ms.
Bierman, and the audience know, that if you expect me to roll
around in the mud with you, I'm not going to do it. You think
the Governor is weak of mind, Reverand? That's your opinion
and you're entitled to it, but he travels around this country with
views, the same views, which he alters for no one, not for

Democratic or progressive groups, not for Republican or conservative his groups, and not for you. Calling him a Rino because he's not afraid to take the heat by expressing views he knows won't always be popular, is not weakness, it's strength. Anyone can be a sheep. Anyone can go with the flow. You and he have more in common than he does with anyone on this panel. He thinks abortion is a terrible thing, but he cannot make the decision for a woman carrying a baby. That woman needs to make that decision, I hope, with the advice and love from the father and those close to her. He doesn't agree with abortion in many cases, but he's not in the position that a pregnant woman is in. She will have to live with the decision." It's easy to call other people names. In politics, it's practically expected, but that doesn't mean he has to it. I can tell you, right to your face or anybody else's, whether I agree with your opinion or not, and where you have common ground. The Reverand said nothing, and Dan continued. While he has said repeatedly that he does not care to attack people on a personal level, but to attack ideas, the fact that this Ms. Simon here finds jubilation in abortion disgusts me. We both believe in treating everyone with respect, that is, until they cross the line. Ms. Baxter here, you may not agree on this or other topics, but I can respect your opinion. The opinion of Ms. Simon, I cannot find any respect for. There comes a time when a person's opinion is so vile that it defines them, and then there is no separation between an opinion and a person's character. Ms. Simon, you are a disgusting human being." There was a clear murmur from the audience, a few chuckles. Then, not surprisingly came the response from Wendy Simon. "Oh, eat me, you AND Greenbaum are Zionist pigs." Then the audience erupted. A few claps, a few laughs, but mostly just a gasp of disbelief. It was THE soundbite of the show, exactly what Melissa wanted. Clearly, Simon practiced that line well before the show, forgetting the fact that Dan Bennet, not Milt Greenbaum, was on the panel, and he wasn't Jewish, but certainly, you could be a Zionist without being Jewish, so the comment stayed. Speaking of jubilation, this was it. Out from her earpiece, from the control room, came a loud "Bingo!" But, of course, Melissa Bierman, had to step in. "C'mon Wendy. Zionist? Aren't you Jewish yourself?" "So, what, said Simon. "That doesn't mean I support an apartheid government." "Okay", said Bierman, who was, ironically and maybe even comically, also Jewish. "Let's save the Middle East discussion for another show." There was no quieting down the audience now.

The show ended with Dan shaking hands with Bierman, Joan Baxter, and yes, even the Reverand, after Dan stuck his hand out. Everybody hated Wendy Simon, even Joan Baxter, even Melissa Bierman, and even most liberal Americans, who stopped short of displaying a "love" for abortion. But Melissa Bierman had absolutely no regrets bringing her on the show.

Needless to say, the show was the talk of social media, though Milt, as usual, failed to really move the needle. Some respected his honesty and ability to stand firm, even if many others had to agree that nice or not, the Reverand wasn't wrong in calling him a "RINO". His stance on abortion simply wasn't in step with most Republicans, or at least that what the prevailing thought was. If anything, it was Democrats, in general that believed his comments to be reasonable, but reasonable or not, while some did indeed vote based on one issue, many others did not, and they wouldn't cast a vote for a Republican, no matter what."

But the "RINO" comment, while used before, simply added insult to injury, another seed planted in the minds of Republicans that a President Greenbaum would "cave" to the leftist Democrats, whether Greenbaum called it compromise or not. They didn't care about "reaching across the aisle". Neither side generally did, and even those in office who knew that was best, wouldn't risk their seat to do it.

Joan Baxer, the advocate for woman's rights, came out looking bland, but she wasn't used to being on center stage, and she wasn't even mentioned by most groups discussing the show on

the many social media sites. For that, she was glad. But Joan
Baxer wasn't running for President, Milton Greenbaum was, and
if he had one foot firmly planted in a political "no man's land",
he was rolling around in it, now.

# Wrap-Up

Madison stuck to the Republican talking points, and he won the necessary delegates to secure the nomination, held, ironically, at the State Farm Arena in downtown Atlanta. The two men shook hands on the stage and Milt promised to support his run, just like a good party member.

Milt took another sip from his Summer Shandy, a gift from Dan, six cases of the lemonade-inspired beer that had now hooked Milt from his house on Lake Lanier. Would the Leinenkugel people support his candidacy? Who knows? They just make great beer for everybody. Milt would never know and didn't want to know. He liked that.  Maybe someday he'd find a place on Lake Wissota, near their brewery in Chippewa Falls. He could certainly afford it. He looked over the lake, Lake Lanier, a little tired and, frankly, a little melancholy. Just then, the phone rang. It was three days before Halloween, and he didn't feel like attending any little parties at the Governor's mansions. Besides, he would be out of that job in a matter of weeks, handing the rein over to Bill Adams, a local Atlanta businessman and Georgia Tech graduate who stayed out of trouble and towed the Republican line for the most part. Milt liked him and they met for a meeting and to hand off the torch. It's funny, because in 1996, it was the other way around. Both Milt and Bill participated in the Atlanta Olympics running of the torch, and Bill handed off the torch to Milt. Milt ran his route into midtown, and then four runners later, the torch was passed off to Olympic great Al Oerter, four-time discuss gold medalist, who ran into the lower part of the stadium, and handed the torch to Evander Holyfield. He had the honor of bringing the torch up into the stadium, where he received a huge ovation. He later passed it off to swimmer Janet Evans, but the lighting of the torch fell to Muhammad Ali, and it became one of the great moments in Olympic history.

Milt picked up the phone. "Can't you let a defeated man dry his tears in peace?" "Oh, c'mon, now", said Dan. "You did what you set out to do, didn't you?" "I don't know", said Milt. "Did I? I was taught at Memphis that there was no such thing as a moral victory." "Well, I don't believe that, not really," said Dan. You and I sat in a lot of courtrooms. We tried to do what was right. We didn't always succeed, but you know, we must sleep at night, and live a good life. Isn't that a victory in itself?" "Losing isn't victory, Dan", a resolute Milt said, not sure if he believed his own words. I hoped that the nation could do it right this time." "Well," Dan answered, "what they want vs what you think they should want are two different things. That's what makes America great, and in spite of all the crap trying to weigh us down, to scuttle the ship, the corruption, the lies, the cheating, all of it, Milt, and you don't have to be a conspiracy nut to know that it all goes on, in spite of it all, it's a great country. It's great despite the celebrities that swear they'll leave if they don't get their way. It's great despite the riots, the meltdowns, the stupidity, the unwillingness to compromise. The Constitution is like that aircraft carrier, the Yorktown, beaten, but not down. It seems to survive despite all the attempts to render it useless, dead in the water. I don't know how, Milt, but we survived. Maybe someday, it'll be too much, and we'll sink from the damage. Probably so, but not yet. You're an honorable man, a respected man, and maybe the country isn't ready to get back to your methods, compromise, character, civility. Hell, Milt, I watched the Kennedy-Nixon debate tape, and they practically got along compared to the mudslinging of today. The country wants what they want, and they want crusty old men who can't find a nice word to say, or maybe can't remember what they even said last, but support their beliefs, and at the end of the day, that's who you vote for, the person that best supports your beliefs. The system works, warts and all. I thought you were right, Milt. I believed in you, and you can hold your head up high."

"Thanks, Dan," Milt said, and Milt simply had no response for Dan right now. Sometimes, remaining silent is the best response. He had too many thoughts swimming around in his mind. "So," Dan asked. "What are you going to do now?" "I don't know," said Milt. Finish my beer, then have another one. Listen to music. Doing nothing sounds good to me right now, but at some point, I'll get involved in something. It won't be politics. I won't run again. I said my peace so maybe I'll volunteer for something. Maybe move to Wisconsin." "Wisconsin? Dan was surprised, only because Milt had never mentioned it before." "I'm just kidding, though I hear Chippewa Falls is pretty. I'll take some time off and think about it. I have a lot of time.

The election was less than two weeks away, and Milt would have to drive down to Atlanta to vote. He had never missed an election. It was an obligation as a citizen to him, even if he had to, at times, hold his nose while casting his vote. He thought of the millions who never could vote, for different reasons, and realized that despite it all, he wasn't in such a bad place in his life. He had the opportunity to go for the brass ring because he lived here. Nobody told him he would grab it, but at least, Milt thought while taking another sip of his Summer Shandy, he was given the chance.

Election night was long, and the outcome wasn't certain until after midnight on that Tuesday, but nobody was thinking about Milt Greenbaum, because Steve Madison was facing off against the Democratic challenger. There were three debates, with the same tired arguments in the mix. One side talking about the right to a free education, the right to free healthcare, the right for minorities to receive special treatment, and the privilege of the majority that kept them from understanding the plight of those less privileged than them. Change must take place, for people, for the planet, for the sake of making people feel less threatened, less hurt, and the way for that to happen was to allow the government to have greater power. This was the way for America to be great.

The other side stuck to its talking points, how the Founding Fathers developed an amazing system that today gave everyone the opportunity to thrive, that personal responsibility was the key. Work hard, work smart, and take responsibility, and anything was possible.

After the inauguration, Milt was a guest on Jim Martin's show, "Political Madness", which was as much a comedy show than anything else. Martin got into the business as a comic, but always talked about politics, and eventually got a cable show and then his current show. He specialized in putting all kinds of celebrities on his program, with different political views, on the show to argue and laugh. Sure, things got a little out of control at times, but he seemed to get everyone, politicians, athletes, entertainers, mostly. He was known more as a liberal but just when you thought you knew him, and what he might say, he went the other way. He had balls, that much was for sure.

So, Milt was the only guest, and Jim began by asking a bold question, "C'mon, Governor, Major, whatever you want to be called, you're a smart guy, did you ever think you could be a middle of the road candidate and not get squashed? Remember Mr. Miyagi and The Karate Kid?" "Sure, I do", said Milt. "Well, to paraphrase one of his quotes, "Walk right side, safe. Walk left side, safe. Walk middle, sooner or later, you get squished just like grape. Here karate the same thing. But instead, that's politics."

"No, I didn't think I would win, but I kept out hope for America, that they would listen to common sense, to reason." "Why? Americans want what they want," Martin answered. "Whoever gave the credit for making smart choices?" The got a laugh from

the audience. "Well,", Milt said, "You can blame the politicians."
"Oh?", smirked Martin. "Ya think?" The audience laughed.
"Yeah", Milt said, taking on the challenge. "I do think".
Politicians must have the division for the sake of their own
power, staying in power in office. The more division, the better.
So, that means the right policies aren't passed. There may be
compromise in Congress, but none of the policies are right for
the American people. Or many, anyway, and the people begin
to believe in ridiculous notions, fed by the politicians, to egg
them on." There was some applause.

Martin spoke, "Remember when the President was looked up
to, when every little boy wanted to grow up to be President? Of
course, little girls didn't dare dream that, but now they can.
Now it's in reach, so Governor, what should we expect from a
President? I don't mean anything that's related to a specific
policy, but in general. After all, you ran on a platform, and
wrote a book called "Common Sense"?

"Well,", Milt began. I was one of those kids who dreamed of
becoming President. I dreamed of being a leader. Somebody
who the nation looked at to do the right things. When I was ten,
I was dreaming of an agenda, an economic or foreign policy. No,
it was fare vaguer. But I envisioned myself looking the part,
down to being neatly dressed. Respecting the office. Not having
sex with women who aren't called 'First Lady', in the oval office
or in the White House. Not calling the opposition names like a
2nd grader. Not taking millions in payola from other nations. I
envisioned saving the country. Being a leader. Somebody the
country could listen to and feel better if times were tough.

Since then, I'm less naïve, but why <u>shouldn't</u> the President be
somebody we could admire and respect?  First, the President
must protect and defend the Constitution, the document with
our most basic freedoms is written. This is why the President
swears upon a Bible to do just that. Before we worry about new

taxes, or social programs, will they protect our basic freedoms? Some say yes, but we've got to hold them to it.

Next, will they physically defend our shores? Keep us strong. You and I could have two completely different personalities and outlooks on politics, but if we're not safe walking down the street, nothing else would matter. We need a strong military, and we need a network of police officers who will protect and serve, responsibly. If we don't have that, we need to replace people. We don't need to get rid of the service, just the bad apples. So, number two, we need physical protection.

We need a strong economy. We're a market-driven economy. A Capitalistic system. That must be always kept in mind. The private sector cannot run rampant. It needs checks and balances. It needs oversight, and it needs compromise, but it also needs to be protected.

Finally, and there are other areas, but I'll just say that we've had our share of characters in the Oval Office. Some have been loud, some are too quiet, some have strange family members. The President is supposed represent the "best of the best". We'd like a President who is intelligent, who is articulate, who is intelligent, and why not? This is the highest office in the land. We don't want or need an absentminded, impolite person who can't control themselves or remember things. We've had too much of that lately, on both sides.

In our entire great nation, of ivy-covered halls, great orators, men and women of business, of law, of medicine, of science, in the arts. Great military leaders. This is the best of the best? This is what represents the land of Lincoln, the majestic Rockies, the magnificent Pacific, the awe-inspiring sites of Yellowstone, Glacier National Park, and Yosemite?" "Ok, Shakespeare." Jim Martin had to inject some comedy into the show. Milt's comments were getting a little too thick for the show" The audience chuckled, and seemed to appreciate the break, but at the same time, Milt really struck a chord. This is the best we can do?

"Okay", said Martin. "I asked you to make ten straight comments, political or social comments, before today, that you could read out, showing the stupidity of the American people." "Stubbornness", said Milt. "I'm not saying stupid." "Oh, fuck that!" yelled Martin, but with a smile. "Not on my show, Governor. They're stupid, all right.

So, let's hear the statements. This is for the ages. It'll be played back for a very long time, so don't be nervous. More laughter. We asked you to make one statement. One defining sentence on the topic, and then three or four sentences providing some detail. Milt cleared his throat. "Ok, here we go.

1. <u>No system is better than Capitalism</u>. We might be a blend of Capitalism and socialism, but it's only because of a strong Capitalistic system that we can absorb the social programs, the Socialism piece. It can't be 50-50, but more like 80-20. No system is fairer than Capitalism and helps more people, even though, it has corruption, but never, ever as destructive as Socialism, which lowers the bar, removes competition and motivation, and makes politicians more corrupt than under any under system. It never works and never will work and it's the opposite of everything America was founded on and stands for."

2. <u>Our border must be secure.</u> We are a country of immigrants, and we want immigration. But the border is wide open so that these illegal aliens, and that's what they are, can drain our system and being Democratic voters. Once again, the politicians are only interested in their own power and riches, and most could not care less about the future of this country.

103

3.  <u>Gay people deserve the same rights as everybody, so let's move on</u>. Gay people were born that way. When did you decide to be straight? Why are people so stupid? Because they fall back on religion and are scared to use common sense. People are gay because of something in their brains, call it wiring or something else. It's not psychological. It's not a mental illness. It is a physical difference of some kind vs. heterosexuals. Of course, if everyone was gay, the population would disappear, but that will never be the case because gay people are in the minority, but there's a lot of them, and there always HAS been, so let's move on. Give them all the same rights, and let's find real problems to solve.

4.  <u>Transgender people have nothing to do with gay people and we still need to work on this topic</u>. They believe that they are something they are not. Chromosomes are rock solid. There are several other characteristics, but chromosomes are factual and cannot be changed. So, it's not physical. It's mental. Mental illness? A mental condition, anyway. The numbers are small. Get them treatment. If they are adults and want to live as another sex, well, they're adults. Don't demean them any more than you would somebody who was schizophrenic. Be nice, but don't change public policy that serves the majority because of a few transgenders. Men's bathrooms are for men, and women's for women. If a man wears a dress and looks enough like a woman, do you let them use the men's bathroom? That falls under the area of "Hell, I don't know." Politicians are seen as weak for saying that. Do you force a man wearing a dress into a men's bathroom, where they will look equally stupid? I don't know. I never said I had all the answers.

But this concept of people saying they can't define a woman for you, and then expect us to allow them to sit on the bench of the Supreme Court, of stand there and explain that a woman can have a penis, or a man can get pregnant. That's just moronic, and it needs to stop, and people in the public eye say it should be ridiculed, because it's stupid. Did you hear me, America? It's stupid. And do not allow a transgender woman into women's sports until we know more, if ever. They have too many physical advantages."

5.  Climate change. <u>Climate change must be open for discussion and dissenting opinions.</u> This is one of those topics where people have decided if you even question the leftist opinion, you're less than human. In the meantime, professors can't publish papers if they don't go along with the status quo. There has always been climate changed. The ice age lasted well over 2 million years. So, the temperature is rising. Everybody can agree on that. Nothing we can do to change solar patterns. But many say humans are responsible. After all, look at all the crap we've thrown up into the atmosphere. If I filled a room with smoke, you would die, so this human change is possible, but experts can't agree. Then you've got politicians getting involved, for power and riches, like always. Scientists' can's question like they're supposed to do. They can't have dissenting positions, or they're ostracized. What is the answer? Let's look for it and see if change can be implemented without destroying our way of life. There is always room for another opinion. Oil is messy and one day we'll have better energy sources. Keep working toward them, but they must be able to be marketed effectively, at a profit, and in demand at a fair price. Don't force products and services down the public's throats.

6.  <u>Abortion. Abortion can and probably should stay legal, but it is still the death of living human, and we should work much harder to minimize its occurrence.</u>

It's an unfortunate, terrible thing, but still, the choice should lie with the woman. There will never be a way to reach a peaceful resolution on this topic. It's nothing to celebrate or gloat about. Maybe a new over-the-counter contraceptive will help. It saddens me and I wish nobody ever felt the need to do it, and that's all I can say.

Milt Greenbaum's grand experiment failed. He spent his remaining years dabbling in real estate, traveling, and helping organizations like the Kiwanis Club in the Atlanta area. In the end, the people decided what they wanted, and Milt wondered if a country as great as America only has a certain number of years to work well, until the people decide they don't want to fight for liberty, and it goes the way of other great civilizations.

But thanks to a pendant for selling meat, cheese, and other assorted groceries, Milt would live the "American Dream", until his demise at the age of 92. Several books were written after his death, as well as a popular Netflix documentary that explored his life and candidacy, called "Common Sense: The Milt Greenbaum story".  Some people wondered, after the fact, if America's greatness was finally dead after the country rejected the common sense of Milt Greenbaum, and continued down their road to destruction, unlike, perhaps, the Roman Empire, but with similar results.

The election over, and life went on. Funny that. With all the doomsday predictions. "The most important election the nation has ever faced". Life in America still went on, and Milt took a little time off to decide what he might do next. He didn't have to work but that wasn't Milt's way. Offers from law firms were already coming in. He'd take six months to relax and see.

It was a fine October Saturday, and Milt was invited to watch Ole Miss play LSU, always a very tough opponent, but nothing ever detracted from the party on the "Grove" on the Ole Miss campus, where Milt was invited by some Memphis friends. As they liked to say in Oxford, "We might lose the game, but we never lost the party", and they didn't.

It was early evening on Saturday when Milt drive west on 278, through Batesville, for the easy one-hour drive to Clarksdale. He was invited to a church service, even though he was pretty sure the Minister didn't vote for him.

He had a 4:00 flight back to Atlanta, from Memphis, but before he left, he stopped at the Rest Haven for a piece of chocolate pie, hoping he wouldn't be noticed under his Memphis Tigers cap. But he couldn't fool Helen, the waitress, who recognized him right away, but understood and kept her cool. Why Governor Greenbaum, nice to see you back in Clarksdale. What brings you here? Milt took a forkful of that delicious chocolate pie, lifted it toward Helen, and said, "Well, I needed a taste of the simple life." Governor or not, Helen responded as Helen always did. "I understand, honey."

# APPENDIX

# Preamble to the Constitution

**We the People** of the United States, in order to form a more perfect union, establish <u>justice</u>, insure domestic

tranquility, provide for the common defense, promote
the general welfare, and secure the blessings of liberty
to ourselves and our posterity, <u>do ordain and establish
this Constitution for the United States of America.</u>

## Article. I.

## Section. 1.

All legislative powers herein granted shall be vested in a
congress of the United States, which shall consist of
a <u>Senate and House of Representatives</u>.

## Section. 2.

The <u>House of Representatives</u> shall be composed of
members chosen every second year by the people of
the several states, and the electors in each state shall
have the qualifications requisite for electors of the most
numerous branch of the state legislature.

No person shall be a representative who shall not have
attained to the age of twenty-five years and been seven
years a citizen of the United States, and who shall not,
when elected, be an inhabitant of that state in which he
shall be chosen.

Representatives and direct taxes shall be apportioned among the several States which may be included within this union, according to their respective numbers, which shall be determined by adding to the whole number of free persons, including those bound to service for a term of years, and excluding Indians not taxed, three fifths of all other persons. The actual enumeration shall be made within three years after the first meeting of the Congress of the United States, and within every subsequent term of ten years, in such manner as they shall by law direct. The number of representatives shall not exceed one for every thirty thousand, but each state shall have at least one representative; and until such enumeration shall be made, the state of New Hampshire shall be entitled to chose three, Massachusetts eight, Rhode-Island and Providence Plantations one, Connecticut five, New-York six, New Jersey four, Pennsylvania eight, Delaware one, Maryland six, Virginia ten, North Carolina five, South Carolina five, and Georgia three.

When vacancies happen in the representation from any state, the Executive authority thereof shall issue writs of election to fill such vacancies.

The House of Representatives shall choose their speaker and other officers; and shall have the sole power of impeachment.

## Section. 3.

The <u>Senate</u> of the United States shall be composed of two Senators from each State, <u>chosen by the Legislature</u> thereof, for six years; and each Senator shall have one Vote.

Immediately after they shall be assembled in consequence of the first Election, they shall be divided as equally as may be into three classes. The seats of the Senators of the first class shall be vacated at the expiration of the second year, of the second class at the expiration of the fourth year, and of the third class at the expiration of the sixth year, so that one third may be chosen every second year; and if vacancies happen by resignation, or otherwise, during the recess of the legislature of any state, the executive thereof may make temporary appointments until the next meeting of the legislature, which shall then fill such vacancies.

No person shall be a Senator who shall not have attained to the age of thirty years and been nine years a citizen of the United States, and who shall not, when elected, be an inhabitant of that state for which he shall be chosen.

The Vice President of the United States shall be President of the Senate, but shall have no vote, unless they be equally divided.

The Senate shall choose their other officers, and also a President pro tempore, in the absence of the Vice President, or when he shall exercise the Office of President of the United States.

The Senate shall have the sole power to try all <u>impeachments</u>. When sitting for that purpose, they shall be on oath or affirmation. When the President of the United States is tried, the Chief Justice shall preside: And no person shall be convicted without the concurrence of two thirds of the members present.

Judgment in cases of impeachment shall not extend further than to removal from Office, and disqualification to hold and enjoy any office of honor, trust or profit under the United States: but the party convicted shall nevertheless be liable and subject to indictment, trial, judgment and punishment, according to law.

## Section. 4.

The times, places and manner of holding elections
for <u>Senators and Representatives</u>, shall be prescribed in
each state by the legislature thereof; but the Congress
may at any time by law make or alter such regulations,
except as to the places of choosing Senators.

The Congress shall assemble at least once in every year,
and such meeting shall be on <u>the first Monday in
December</u>, unless they shall by law appoint a different
Day.

## Section. 5.

Each House shall be the judge of the elections, returns
and qualifications of its own members, and a majority of
each shall constitute a quorum to do business; but a
smaller number may adjourn from day to day, and may
be authorized to compel the attendance of absent
members, in such manner, and under such penalties as
each House may provide.

Each House may determine the rules of its <u>proceedings</u>,
punish its members for disorderly behavior, and, with
the concurrence of two thirds, expel a member.

Each House shall keep a Journal of its proceedings, and from time to time publish the same, excepting such parts as may in their judgment require secrecy; and the yeas and nays of the members of either house on any question shall, at the desire of one fifth of those present, be entered on the journal.

Neither House, during the session of <u>Congress</u>, shall, without the consent of the other, adjourn for more than three days, nor to any other place than that in which the two Houses shall be sitting.

## Section. 6.

The Senators and Representatives shall receive a Compensation for their Services, to be ascertained by law, and paid out of the Treasury of the United States. They shall in all cases, except treason, felony and breach of the peace, be privileged from arrest during their attendance at the session of their respective <u>Houses</u>, and in going to and returning from the same; and for any speech or debate in either, they shall not be questioned in any other place.

No Senator or Representative shall, during the time for which he was elected, be appointed to any civil office under the authority of the United States, which shall have been created, or the emoluments whereof shall have been increased during such time; and no person holding any office under the United States, shall be a member of either House during his continuance in office.

## Section. 7.

All Bills for <u>raising revenue</u> shall originate in the House of Representatives; but the Senate may propose or concur with amendments as on other Bills.

Every bill which shall have passed the House of Representatives and the Senate, shall, before it become a law, be presented to the <u>President</u> of the United States; If he approve he shall sign it, but if not he shall return it, with his objections to that House in which it shall have originated, who shall enter the objections at large on their journal, and proceed to reconsider it. If after such reconsideration two thirds of that House shall agree to pass the bill, it shall be sent, together with the objections, to the other House, by which it shall likewise be reconsidered, and if approved by two thirds of that House, it shall become a law. But in all such cases the votes of both houses shall be determined by yeas and nays, and the names of the persons voting for and against the bill shall be entered on the journal of each house respectively. If any bill shall not be returned by the President within ten days (Sundays excepted) after it shall have been presented to him, the same shall be a law, in like manner as if he had signed it, unless the Congress by their adjournment prevent its return, in which case it shall not be a law.

Every order, resolution, or vote to which the concurrence of the Senate and House of Representatives may be necessary (except on a question of Adjournment) shall be presented to the President of the United States; and before the same shall take effect, shall be approved by him, or being disapproved by him, shall be repassed by two thirds of the Senate and House of Representatives, according to the rules and limitations prescribed in the Case of a Bill.

## Section. 8.

The Congress shall have power to lay and collect taxes, duties, imposts and excises, to pay the debts and provide for the common defence and general welfare of the United States; but all duties, imposts and excises shall be uniform throughout the United States;

To borrow money on the credit of the United States.

To regulate _commerce_ with foreign nations, and among the several states, and with the Indian Tribes;

To establish an uniform Rule of _Naturalization_, and uniform Laws on the subject of Bankruptcies throughout the United States;

To coin money, regulate the value thereof, and of foreign coin, and fix the standard of weights and measures.

To provide for the punishment of counterfeiting the securities and current coin of the United States.

To establish Post Offices and post roads.

To promote the progress of science and useful arts, by securing for limited times to authors and _inventors_ the exclusive right to their respective writings and discoveries;

To constitute tribunals inferior to the Supreme Court.

To define and punish piracies and felonies committed on the high seas, and offences against the Law of Nations.

To declare <u>war</u>, grant letters of marque and reprisal, and make rules concerning captures on land and water;

To raise and support armies, but no appropriation of money to that use shall be for a longer term than two years.

To provide and maintain a navy.

To make rules for the government and regulation of the land and naval forces.

To provide for calling forth the militia to execute the laws of the Union, suppress insurrections and repel invasions.

To provide for organizing, arming, and disciplining, the militia, and for governing such part of them as may be employed in the service of the United States, reserving to the states respectively, the appointment of the officers, and the authority of training the militia according to the discipline prescribed by Congress.

To exercise exclusive Legislation in all cases whatsoever, over such district (not exceeding ten miles square) as may, by cession of particular states, and the acceptance of Congress, become the seat of the government of the United States, and to exercise like authority over all places purchased by the consent of the legislature of the State in which the same shall be, for the erection of forts, magazines, arsenals, dock-yards, and other needful buildings;—And

To make all laws which shall be <u>necessary and proper</u> for carrying into execution the foregoing powers, and all other powers vested by this Constitution in the Government of the United States, or in any department or officer thereof.

## Section. 9.

The migration or <u>importation of such Persons</u> as any of the States now existing shall think proper to admit, shall not be prohibited by the Congress prior to the year one thousand eight hundred and eight, but a tax or duty may be imposed on such importation, not exceeding ten dollars for each person.

The Privilege of the Writ of Habeas Corpus shall not be suspended, unless when in cases of rebellion or invasion the public safety may require it.

No bill of attainder or ex post facto law shall be passed.

No Capitation, or other direct, tax shall be laid, <u>unless in Proportion to the Census or enumeration herein before directed to be taken.</u>

No tax or duty shall be laid on articles exported from any state.

No preference shall be given by any regulation of commerce or revenue to the ports of one state over those of another: nor shall vessels bound to, or from, one state, be obliged to enter, clear, or pay duties in another.

No money shall be drawn from the Treasury, but in consequence of appropriations made by law; and a regular statement and account of the receipts and expenditures of all public money shall be published from time to time.

No title of nobility shall be granted by the United States: And no person holding any office of profit or trust under them, shall, without the consent of the Congress, accept of any present, emolument, office, or title, of any kind whatever, from any King, Prince, or foreign State.

**Section. 10.**

No state shall enter into any treaty, alliance, or confederation; grant letters of marque and reprisal; coin money; emit bills of credit; make any thing but gold and silver coin a tender in payment of debts; pass any bill of attainder, ex post facto law, or law impairing the obligation of contracts, or grant any Title of Nobility.

No state shall, without the consent of the Congress, lay any imposts or duties on imports or exports, except what may be absolutely necessary for executing it's inspection laws: and the net produce of all duties and imposts, laid by any state on imports or exports, shall be for the use of the Treasury of the United States; and all such laws shall be subject to the revision and control of the Congress.

No state shall, without the consent of Congress, lay any duty of tonnage, keep troops, or ships of war in time of peace, enter into any agreement or compact with another state, or with a foreign power, or engage in war, unless actually invaded, or in such imminent danger as will not admit of delay.

**Article. II.**

**Section. 1.**

The <u>executive</u> power shall be vested in a President of the United States of America. He shall hold his office during the term of four years, and, together with the Vice President, chosen for the same term, be elected, as follows.

Each state shall appoint, in such manner as the Legislature thereof may direct, a Number of Electors, equal to the whole number of Senators and Representatives to which the state may be entitled in the Congress: but no Senator or Representative, or person holding an office of trust or profit under the United States, shall be appointed an elector.

The Electors shall meet in their respective states, and vote by ballot for two persons, of whom one at least shall not be an inhabitant of the same state with themselves. And they shall make a list of all the persons voted for, and of the number of votes for each, which list they shall sign and certify, and transmit sealed to the seat of the government of the United States, directed to the President of the Senate. The President of the Senate shall, in the presence of the Senate and House of Representatives, open all the certificates, and the votes shall then be counted. The person having the greatest number of votes shall be the President, if such number be a majority of the whole number of electors appointed; and if there be more than one who have such majority, and have an equal number of votes, then the House of Representatives shall immediately chose by ballot one of them for President; and if no person have a majority, then from the five highest on the list the said house shall in like manner chose the President. But in choosing the President, the votes shall be taken by states, the representation from each state having one vote; A quorum for this purpose shall consist of a member or members from two thirds of the states, and a majority of all the states shall be necessary to a choice. In every case, after the choice of the President, the person having the greatest number of votes of the electors shall be the Vice President. But if there should remain two or more who have equal votes, the Senate shall chose from them by ballot the Vice President.

The Congress may determine the time of choosing the electors, and the day on which they shall give their votes, which day shall be the same throughout the United States.

No person except a natural born citizen, or a citizen of the United States, at the time of the adoption of this Constitution, shall be eligible to the Office of President; neither shall any person be eligible to that office who shall not have attained to the age of thirty five years, and been fourteen years a resident within the United States.

In case of the removal of the President from office, or of his death, resignation, or inability to discharge the powers and duties of the said office, the same shall devolve on the Vice President, and the Congress may by law provide for the case of removal, death, resignation or inability, both of the President and Vice President, declaring what officer shall then act as President, and such officer shall act accordingly, until the disability be removed, or a President shall be elected.

The President shall, at stated times, receive for his services, a Compensation, which shall neither be increased nor diminished during the period for which he shall have been elected, and he shall not receive within that period any other emolument from the United States, or any of them.

Before he <u>enter on the Execution of his Office, he shall take the following Oath or Affirmation</u>:—"I do solemnly swear (or affirm) that I will faithfully execute the Office of <u>President of the United States</u>, and will to the best of my Ability, preserve, protect and defend the Constitution of the United States."

## Section. 2.

The President shall be <u>Commander in Chief</u> of the Army and Navy of the United States, and of the militia of the several States, when called into the actual service of the United States; he may require the opinion, in writing, of the principal officer in each of the executive departments, upon any subject relating to the duties of their respective offices, and he shall have power to grant <u>reprieves and pardons</u> for offences against the United States, except in cases of impeachment.

He shall have power, by and with the <u>advice and consent of the Senate</u>, to make <u>treaties</u>, provided two thirds of the Senators present concur; and he shall nominate, and by and with the advice and consent of the Senate, shall appoint ambassadors, other public ministers and consuls, judges of the supreme court, and all other Officers of the United States, whose appointments are not herein otherwise provided for, and which shall be established by law: but the Congress may by law vest the appointment of such inferior officers, as they think proper, in the President alone, in the courts of law, or in the heads of departments.

The President shall have power to fill up all vacancies that may happen during the recess of the Senate, by granting commissions which shall expire at the end of their next session.

## Section. 3.

He shall from time to time give to the Congress Information of the State of the Union, and recommend to their Consideration such Measures as he shall judge necessary and expedient; he may, on extraordinary Occasions, convene both Houses, or either of them, and in Case of Disagreement between them, with Respect to the Time of Adjournment, he may adjourn them to such Time as he shall think proper; he shall receive Ambassadors and other public Ministers; he shall take Care that the laws be faithfully executed, and shall Commission all the Officers of the United States.

## Section. 4.

The President, Vice President and all civil Officers of the United States, shall be removed from Office on <u>impeachment</u> for, and conviction of, treason, bribery, or other high crimes and misdemeanors.

## Article III.

### Section. 1.

The <u>judicial power</u> of the United States, shall be vested in one Supreme Court, and in such inferior courts as the Congress may from time to time ordain and establish. The judges, both of the supreme and inferior courts, shall hold their Offices during good behavior, and shall, at stated times, receive for their services, a compensation, which shall not be diminished during their continuance in Office.

### Section. 2.

The judicial Power shall extend to all <u>cases</u>, in law and equity, arising under this Constitution, the laws of the United States, and treaties made, or which shall be made, under their authority;—to all cases affecting ambassadors, other public ministers and consuls;—to all cases of admiralty and maritime jurisdiction;—to controversies to which the United States shall be a

party;—to controversies between two or more states;—
between a state and citizens of another State,—
between citizens of different States,—between citizens
of the same state claiming lands under grants of
different states, and between a state, or the citizens
thereof, and <u>foreign states,</u> citizens or subjects.

In all Cases affecting Ambassadors, other public
Ministers and Consuls, and those in which a State shall
be Party, the supreme Court shall have original
Jurisdiction. In all the other Cases before mentioned, the
supreme Court shall have appellate Jurisdiction, both as
to Law and Fact, with such Exceptions, and under such
Regulations as the Congress shall make.

The Trial of all Crimes, except in Cases of Impeachment,
shall be by <u>jury</u>; and such Trial shall be held in the State
where the said Crimes shall have been committed; but
when not committed within any State, the Trial shall be
at such Place or Places as the Congress may by Law
have directed.

**Section. 3.**

<u>Treason</u> against the United States, shall consist only in
levying War against them, or in adhering to their

Enemies, giving them Aid and Comfort. No Person shall be convicted of Treason unless on the Testimony of two Witnesses to the same overt Act, or on Confession in open Court.

The Congress shall have Power to declare the Punishment of Treason, but no Attainder of Treason shall work Corruption of Blood, or Forfeiture except during the Life of the Person attainted.

**Article. IV.**

**Section. 1.**

Full Faith and Credit shall be given in each <u>State</u> to the public Acts, Records, and judicial Proceedings of every other State. And the Congress may by general Laws prescribe the Manner in which such Acts, Records and Proceedings shall be proved, and the Effect thereof.

**Section. 2.**

The citizens of each state shall be entitled to all privileges and immunities of citizens in the several states.

A person charged in any State with Treason, Felony, or other Crime, who shall flee from Justice, and be found in another State, shall on Demand of the executive Authority of the State from which he fled, be delivered up, to be removed to the State having Jurisdiction of the Crime.

No Person held to Service or <u>labor</u> in one State, under the Laws thereof, escaping into another, shall, in Consequence of any Law or Regulation therein, be discharged from such Service or labor, but shall be delivered up on Claim of the Party to whom such Service or labor may be due.

**Section. 3.**

New States may be admitted by the Congress into this Union; but no new State shall be formed or erected within the Jurisdiction of any other State; nor any State be formed by the Junction of two or more States, or Parts of States, without the Consent of the Legislatures of the States concerned as well as of the Congress.

The Congress shall have Power to dispose of and make all needful Rules and Regulations respecting the Territory or other Property belonging to the United

States; and nothing in this Constitution shall be so construed as to Prejudice any Claims of the United States, or of any particular State.

**Section. 4.**

The United States shall guarantee to every State in this Union a <u>Republican</u> Form of <u>Government</u>, and shall protect each of them against Invasion; and on Application of the Legislature, or of the Executive (when the Legislature cannot be convened) against domestic Violence.

**Article. V.**

The Congress, whenever two thirds of both Houses shall deem it necessary, shall propose Amendments to this Constitution, or, on the Application of the Legislatures of two thirds of the several States, shall call a Convention for proposing Amendments, which, in either Case, shall be valid to all Intents and Purposes, as Part of this Constitution, when ratified by the Legislatures of three fourths of the several States, or by Conventions in three fourths thereof, as the one or the other Mode of Ratification may be proposed by the Congress; Provided that no Amendment which may be made prior to the

Year One thousand eight hundred and eight shall in any Manner affect the first and fourth Clauses in the Ninth Section of the first Article; and that no State, without its Consent, shall be deprived of its equal Suffrage in the Senate.

## Article. VI.

All Debts contracted and Engagements entered into, before the Adoption of this Constitution, shall be as valid against the United States under this Constitution, as under the Confederation.

This Constitution, and the Laws of the United States which shall be made in Pursuance thereof; and all Treaties made, or which shall be made, under the Authority of the United States, shall be the <u>supreme Law of the Land</u>; and the Judges in every State shall be bound thereby, any Thing in the Constitution or Laws of any State to the Contrary notwithstanding.

The Senators and Representatives before mentioned, and the Members of the several State Legislatures, and all executive and judicial Officers, both of the United States and of the several States, shall be bound by Oath or Affirmation, to support this Constitution; but no <u>religious</u> Test shall ever be required as a Qualification to any Office or public Trust under the United States.

## Article. VII.

The <u>ratification</u> of the Conventions of nine States, shall be sufficient for the Establishment of this Constitution between the States so ratifying the Same.

Done in convention by the unanimous consent of the states present the seventeenth day of September in the year of our Lord one thousand seven hundred and eighty-seven and of the independence of the United States of America the twelfth. <u>In witness whereof We have hereunto subscribed our Names,</u>

**Bill of Rights**

**First Amendment**

*(ratified December 15, 1791)*

Congress shall make no law respecting an establishment of <u>religion</u>, or prohibiting the free exercise thereof; or abridging the <u>freedom of speech,</u> or <u>of the press;</u> or the right of the people peaceably to assemble, and <u>to petition the Government</u> for a redress of grievances.

## Second Amendment

*(ratified December 15, 1791)*

<u>A well-regulated Militia, being necessary to the security of a free State, the right of the people to keep and bear Arms shall not be infringed.</u>

## Third Amendment

*(ratified December 15, 1791)*

No Soldier shall, in time of peace be quartered in any house, without the consent of the Owner, nor in time of war, but in a manner to be prescribed by law.

## Fourth Amendment

*(ratified December 15, 1791)*

The right of the people to be secure in their persons, houses, papers, and effects, against <u>unreasonable searches and seizures</u>, shall not be violated, and no Warrants shall issue, but upon probable cause, supported by Oath or affirmation, and particularly describing the place to be searched, and the persons or things to be seized.

## Fifth Amendment

*(ratified December 15, 1791)*

No person shall be held to answer for a capital, or otherwise infamous crime, unless on a presentment or indictment of a Grand Jury, except in cases arising in the land or naval forces, or in the Militia, when in actual service in time of War or public danger; nor shall any person be subject for the same offence to be twice put in jeopardy of life or limb; nor shall be compelled in any criminal case to be a <u>witness against himself</u>, nor be deprived of life, liberty, or property, without <u>due process</u> of law; nor shall <u>private property</u> be taken for public use, without just compensation.

## Sixth Amendment

*(ratified December 15, 1791)*

In all criminal prosecutions, the accused shall enjoy the right to a speedy and public trial, by an impartial jury of the State and district wherein the crime shall have been committed, which district shall have been previously ascertained by law, and to be informed of the nature and cause of the accusation; to be confronted with the witnesses against him; to have compulsory process for obtaining witnesses in his favor, and to have the Assistance of <u>Counsel</u> for his defense.

## Seventh Amendment

*(ratified December 15, 1791)*

In Suits at common law, where the value in controversy shall exceed twenty dollars, the right of trial by jury shall be preserved, and no fact tried by a jury, shall be otherwise re-examined in any Court of the United States, than according to the rules of the common law.

## Eighth Amendment

*(ratified December 15, 1791)*

Excessive bail shall not be required, nor excessive fines imposed, nor <u>cruel and unusual punishments</u> inflicted.

## Ninth Amendment

*(ratified December 15, 1791)*

<u>The enumeration in the Constitution, of certain rights,
shall not be construed to deny or disparage others
retained by the people.</u>

**Tenth Amendment**

*(ratified December 15, 1791)*

The powers not <u>delegated to the United States by the
Constitution</u>, nor prohibited by it to the States,
are <u>reserved to the States</u> respectively, or to the people.

**Eleventh Amendment**

*Passed by Congress March 4, 1794. Ratified February 7,
1795.*

**Note:** Article III, section 2, of the Constitution was
modified by amendment 11.

The Judicial power of the United States shall not be
construed to extend to any suit in law or equity,
commenced or prosecuted against one of the United
States by Citizens of another State, or by Citizens or
Subjects of any Foreign State.

**Twelfth Amendment**

*Passed by Congress December 9, 1803. Ratified June 15, 1804.*

**Note:** A portion of Article II, section 1 of the Constitution was superseded by the 12th amendment.

The Electors shall meet in their respective states and vote by ballot for President and Vice-President, one of whom, at least, shall not be an inhabitant of the same state with themselves; they shall name in their ballots the person voted for as President, and in distinct ballots the person voted for as Vice-President, and they shall make distinct lists of all persons voted for as President, and of all persons voted for as Vice-President, and of the number of votes for each, which lists they shall sign and certify, and transmit sealed to the seat of the government of the United States, directed to the President of the Senate; — the President of the Senate shall, in the presence of the Senate and House of Representatives, open all the certificates and the votes shall then be counted; — The person having the greatest number of votes for President, shall be the President, if such number be a majority of the whole number of Electors appointed; and if no person have such majority, then from the persons having the highest numbers not exceeding three on the list of those voted for as President, the <u>House of Representatives shall choose immediately, by ballot, the President</u>. But in choosing the President, the votes shall be taken by states, the representation from each state having one vote; a quorum for this purpose shall consist of a member or members from two-thirds of the states, and a majority of all the states shall be necessary to a choice. [And if the House of Representatives shall not choose a President whenever the right of choice shall devolve upon them, before the fourth day of March next following, then the Vice-President shall act as President, as in case of the death or other constitutional disability of the President. –]* The person having the greatest number of votes as Vice-President, shall be the Vice-President, if such number be a majority of the whole number of Electors appointed, and if no person have a majority, then from the two highest numbers on the list, the Senate shall choose the Vice-President; a quorum for the purpose shall consist of two-thirds of the whole number of Senators, and a majority of the whole number shall be necessary to a choice. But no person constitutionally ineligible to the office of President shall be eligible to that of Vice-President of the United

States. *Superseded by section 3 of the 20th amendment.

## Thirteenth Amendment

*Passed by Congress January 31, 1865. Ratified December 6, 1865.*

**Note:** A portion of Article IV, section 2, of the Constitution was superseded by the 13th amendment.

### Section 1.

Neither slavery nor involuntary servitude, except as a punishment for crime whereof the party shall have been duly convicted, shall exist within the United States, or any place subject to their jurisdiction.

### Section 2.

Congress shall have power to enforce this article by appropriate legislation.

## Fourteenth Amendment

*Passed by Congress June 13, 1866. Ratified July 9, 1868.*

**Note:** Article I, section 2, of the Constitution was modified by section 2 of the 14th amendment.

## Section 1.

All persons born or naturalized in the United States, and subject to the jurisdiction thereof, are citizens of the United States and of the State wherein they reside. No State shall make or enforce any law which shall abridge the privileges or immunities of citizens of the United States; nor shall any State deprive any person of life, liberty, or property, without due process of law; nor deny to any person within its jurisdiction the equal protection of the laws.

## Section 2.

Representatives shall be apportioned among the several States according to their respective numbers, counting the whole number of persons in each State, excluding Indians not taxed. But when the right to vote at any election for the choice of electors for President and Vice-President of the United States, Representatives in Congress, the Executive and Judicial officers of a State, or the members of the Legislature thereof, is denied to any of the male inhabitants of such

State, being twenty-one years of age,* and citizens of the United States, or in any way abridged, except for participation in rebellion, or other crime, the basis of representation therein shall be reduced in the proportion which the number of such male citizens shall bear to the whole number of male citizens twenty-one years of age in such State.

**Section 3.**

No person shall be a Senator or Representative in Congress, or elector of President and Vice-President, or hold any office, civil or military, under the United States, or under any State, who, having previously taken an oath, as a member of Congress, or as an officer of the United States, or as a member of any State legislature, or as an executive or judicial officer of any State, to support the Constitution of the United States, shall have engaged in insurrection or rebellion against the same, or given aid or comfort to the enemies thereof. But Congress may by a vote of two-thirds of each House, remove such disability.

**Section 4.**

The validity of the public debt of the United States, authorized by law, including debts incurred for payment of pensions and bounties for services in suppressing insurrection or rebellion, shall not be questioned. But neither the United States nor any State shall assume or pay any debt or obligation incurred in aid of insurrection or rebellion against the United States, or any claim for the loss or emancipation of any slave; but all such debts, obligations and claims shall be held illegal and void.

**Section 5.**

The Congress shall have the power to enforce, by appropriate legislation, the provisions of this article.

*Changed by section 1 of the 26th amendment.*

**Fifteenth Amendment**

*Passed by Congress February 26, 1869. Ratified February 3, 1870.*

**Section 1.**

The right of citizens of the United States to vote shall not be denied or abridged by the United States or by any

State on account of race, color, or previous condition of servitude–

## Section 2.

The Congress shall have the power to enforce this article by appropriate legislation.

## Sixteenth Amendment

*Passed by Congress July 2, 1909. Ratified February 3, 1913.*

**Note:** Article I, section 9, of the Constitution was modified by amendment 16.

<u>The Congress shall have power to lay and collect taxes on incomes,</u> from whatever source derived, without apportionment among the several States, and without regard to any census or enumeration.

## Seventeenth Amendment

*Passed by Congress May 13, 1912. Ratified April 8, 1913.*

**Note:** Article I, section 3, of the Constitution was modified by the 17th amendment.

The Senate of the United States shall be composed of two Senators from each State, elected by the people thereof, for six years; and each Senator shall have one vote. The electors in each State shall have the qualifications requisite for electors of the most numerous branches of the State legislatures.

When vacancies happen in the representation of any State in the Senate, the executive authority of such State shall issue writs of election to fill such vacancies: Provided, That the legislature of any State may empower the executive thereof to make temporary appointments until the people fill the vacancies by election as the legislature may direct.

This amendment shall not be so construed as to affect the election or term of any Senator chosen before it becomes valid as part of the Constitution.

**Eighteenth Amendment**

*Passed by Congress December 18, 1917. Ratified January 16, 1919. Repealed by amendment 21.*

**Section 1.**

After one year from the ratification of this article the manufacture, sale, or transportation of intoxicating liquors within, the importation thereof into, or the exportation thereof from the United States and all territory subject to the jurisdiction thereof for beverage purposes is hereby <u>prohibited.</u>

**Section 2.**

The Congress and the several States shall have concurrent power to enforce this article by appropriate legislation.

**Section 3.**

This article shall be inoperative unless it shall have been ratified as an amendment to the Constitution by the legislatures of the several States, as provided in the Constitution, within seven years from the date of the submission hereof to the States by the Congress.

**Nineteenth Amendment**

*Passed by Congress June 4, 1919. Ratified August 18, 1920.*

The right of citizens of the United States to vote shall not be denied or abridged by the United States or by any State on account of sex.

Congress shall have power to enforce this article by appropriate legislation.

## Twentieth Amendment

*Passed by Congress March 2, 1932. Ratified January 23, 1933.*

**Note:** Article I, section 4, of the Constitution was modified by section 2 of this amendment. In addition, a portion of the 12th amendment was superseded by section 3.

### Section 1.

The terms of the President and the Vice President shall end at noon on the 20th day of January, and the terms of Senators and Representatives at noon on the 3d day of January, of the years in which such terms would have ended if this article had not been ratified; and the terms of their successors shall then begin.

### Section 2.

The Congress shall assemble at least once in every year, and such meeting shall begin at noon on the 3d day of January, unless they shall by law appoint a different day.

## Section 3.

If, at the time fixed for the beginning of the term of the President, the President elect shall have died, the Vice President elect shall become President. If a President shall not have been chosen before the time fixed for the beginning of his term, or if the President elect shall have failed to qualify, then the Vice President elect shall act as President until a President shall have qualified; and the Congress may by law provide for the case wherein neither a President elect nor a Vice President elect shall have qualified, declaring who shall then act as President, or the manner in which one who is to act shall be selected, and such person shall act accordingly until a President or Vice President shall have qualified.

## Section 4.

The Congress may by law provide for the case of the death of any of the persons from whom the House of Representatives may choose a President whenever the right of choice shall have devolved upon them, and for the case of the death of any of the persons from whom the Senate may choose a Vice President whenever the right of choice shall have devolved upon them.

**Section 5.**

Sections 1 and 2 shall take effect on the 15th day of October following the ratification of this article.

**Section 6.**

This article shall be inoperative unless it shall have been ratified as an amendment to the Constitution by the legislatures of three-fourths of the several States within seven years from the date of its submission.

**Twenty-First Amendment**

*Passed by Congress February 20, 1933. Ratified December 5, 1933.*

**Section 1.**

The eighteenth article of amendment to the Constitution of the United States is hereby repealed.

**Section 2.**

The transportation or importation into any State, Territory, or possession of the United States for delivery or use therein of intoxicating liquors, in violation of the laws thereof, is hereby prohibited.

**Section 3.**

This article shall be inoperative unless it shall have been ratified as an amendment to the Constitution by conventions in the several States, as provided in the Constitution, within seven years from the date of the submission hereof to the States by the Congress.

**Twenty-Second Amendment**

*Passed by Congress March 21, 1947. Ratified February 27, 1951.*

**Section 1.**

No person shall be elected to the office of the President more than twice, and no person who has held the office of President, or acted as President, for more than two years of a term to which some other person was elected President shall be elected to the office of the President more than once. But this Article shall not apply to any person holding the office of President when this Article was proposed by the Congress, and shall not prevent any person who may be holding the office of President, or acting as President, during the term within which this Article becomes operative from holding the office of President or acting as President during the remainder of such term.

## Section 2.

This article shall be inoperative unless it shall have been ratified as an amendment to the Constitution by the legislatures of three-fourths of the several States within seven years from the date of its submission to the States by the Congress.

## Twenty-Third Amendment

*Passed by Congress June 16, 1960. Ratified March 29, 1961.*

## Section 1.

The District constituting the seat of Government of the United States shall appoint in such manner as the Congress may direct:

A number of electors of President and Vice President equal to the whole number of Senators and Representatives in Congress to which the District would be entitled if it were a State, but in no event more than the least populous State; they shall be in addition to those appointed by the States, but they shall be considered, for the purposes of the election of President and Vice President, to be electors appointed by a State; and they shall meet in the District and perform such duties as provided by the twelfth article of amendment.

**Section 2.**

The Congress shall have power to enforce this article by appropriate legislation.

**Twenty-Fourth Amendment**

*Passed by Congress August 27, 1962. Ratified January 23, 1964.*

**Section 1.**

The right of citizens of the United States to vote in any primary or other election for President or Vice President, for electors for President or Vice President, or for Senator or Representative in Congress, shall not be denied or abridged by the United States or any State by reason of failure to pay any poll tax or other tax.

## Section 2.

The Congress shall have power to enforce this article by appropriate legislation.

## Twenty-Fifth Amendment

*Passed by Congress July 6, 1965. Ratified February 10, 1967.*

**Note:** Article II, section 1, of the Constitution was affected by the 25th amendment.

## Section 1.

In case of the removal of the President from office or of his death or resignation, the Vice President shall become President.

## Section 2.

Whenever there is a vacancy in the office of the Vice President, the President shall nominate a Vice President

153

who shall take office upon confirmation by a majority vote of both Houses of Congress.

## Section 3.

Whenever the President transmits to the President pro tempore of the Senate and the Speaker of the House of Representatives his written declaration that he is unable to discharge the powers and duties of his office, and until he transmits to them a written declaration to the contrary, such powers and duties shall be discharged by the Vice President as Acting President.

## Section 4.

Whenever the Vice President and a majority of either the principal officers of the executive departments or of such other body as Congress may by law provide, transmit to the President pro tempore of the Senate and the Speaker of the House of Representatives their written declaration that the President is unable to discharge the powers and duties of his office, the Vice President shall immediately assume the powers and duties of the office as Acting President.

Thereafter, when the President transmits to the President pro tempore of the Senate and the Speaker of the House of Representatives his written declaration that no inability exists, he shall resume the powers and duties of his office unless the Vice President and a majority of either the principal officers of the executive department or of such other body as Congress may by law provide, transmit within four days to the President pro tempore of the Senate and the Speaker of the House of Representatives their written declaration that the President is unable to discharge the powers and duties of his office. Thereupon Congress shall decide the issue, assembling within forty-eight hours for that purpose if not in session. If the Congress, within twenty-one days after receipt of the latter written declaration, or, if Congress is not in session, within twenty-one days after Congress is required to assemble, determines by two-thirds vote of both Houses that the President is unable to discharge the powers and duties of his office, the Vice President shall continue to discharge the same as Acting President; otherwise, the President shall resume the powers and duties of his office.

**Twenty-Sixth Amendment**

*Passed by Congress March 23, 1971. Ratified July 1, 1971.*

**Note:** Amendment 14, section 2, of the Constitution was modified by section 1 of the 26th amendment.

**Section 1.**

The right of citizens of the United States, who are eighteen years of age or older, to vote shall not be denied or abridged by the United States or by any State on account of age.

**Section 2.**

The Congress shall have power to enforce this article by appropriate legislation.

**Twenty-Seventh Amendment**

*Originally proposed Sept. 25, 1789. Ratified May 7, 1992.*

No law, varying the compensation for the services of the Senators and Representatives, shall take effect, until an election of Representatives shall have intervened.